SEVEN THE SEARCH OF TH PARLIAMENT

GH01034601

Contents

Preface

For scholars and practitioners of institutional reform of the European Union, the years 1998 and 1999 provide something of a respite. The Treaty of Amsterdam is not yet, as I write, in force. The next intergovernmental conference, intended to coincide somehow with the Union's further enlargement, is still some way off. It is the birth of the euro, and its early life, that commands the agenda today.

What better time (somewhat charged with millenarianism) to step back a little and contemplate the future of parliamentary democracy in a Europe where nation-states seem less fixed and permanent than they once were, and where executive power is more widely dispersed.

The European Parliament, the first directly-elected international parliament in history, is facing its fifth election in June 1999. Yet understanding of the Parliament is generally limited and often ill-judged. Academic research on the Parliament is thin; media attention is spasmodic; the turnout in European Parliamentary elections is low. National perceptions of what the European Parliament is, and should become, vary markedly. MEPs themselves appear to be frustrated: despite the growth of the formal competences of the Parliament over the years, their status is questionable and the reputation of their institution uncertain.

The Federal Trust has set out to enquire what can be done to enhance the representative capability and political credibility of the European Parliament. The study will attempt to identify the strengths and weaknesses of the European Parliament, and will analyse how MEPs might develop their role in the different aspects of the work of the institution, concerning legislation, the budget, scrutiny of the executive, litigation and mediation. Later reports are planned on the role of member state and autonomous regional parliaments within the EU.

We are most grateful to David Coombes for contributing the excellent first of what we expect to be a series of innovative reports on different aspects of representative democracy within the European Union. Michael Steed will act as rapporteur for the whole series. We three are indebted to the several people who commented upon an earlier draft of this paper or helped in other ways, namely: Richard Blackman, Richard Corbett, Harry Cowie, John Fitzmaurice, Christian Franck, Charles

Grant, Francis Jacobs, Thomas Jansen, Karl Magnus Johansson, Bernhard Lamers, Andreas Maurer, David Millar, Gary Miller, Johannes Pollak, Robert Ramsay, Thomas Saalfeld, Michael Shackleton, Otto Schmuck, Julie Smith, Alison Suttie, Andrea Szukala, Anthony Teasdale, Frank Vibert, Martin Westlake and David Williamson.

The Federal Trust welcomes comments on its publications. They should be sent to me at Dean Bradley House, 52 Horseferry Road, London SW1P 2AF.

Andrew Duff

Director

January 1999

About the Author

David Coombes is Professor of European Studies at the University of Limerick in Ireland. He is a Senior Research Fellow of the Federal Trust.

Coombes was previously a Senior Research Fellow at the Policy Studies Institute and Professor of European Studies at Loughborough University. He is the author of many studies of European unification and political institutions, including *Politics and Bureaucracy in the European Community: A Portrait of the Commission of the EEC* (Allen & Unwin, 1970); (ed.) *The Power of the Purse* (Allen & Unwin, 1976), *The Future of the European Parliament* (PSI, 1979); (with S.A. Walkland) *Parliaments and Economic Affairs* (Heinemann, 1981); and *Representative Government and Economic Power* (Heinemann, 1982).

1. 'This Is Not A Parliament'

'A day will come when, by means of a similitude relayed indefinitely along the length of a series, the image itself, along with the name it bears, will lose its identity. Campbell, Campbell, Campbell, Campbell.'

Michel Foucault *This Is Not a Pipe* [1]

What is the European Parliament, and how might it perform better? No good political analyst could honestly say in a simple, straightforward manner what are the answers to these questions. The first and major complication is the difficulty of knowing to what kind of political order, if any, the institution of the European Parliament belongs. Indeed, to explore any political aspect of European Union is very much like an expedition into uncharted territory; we find ourselves perplexed in unfamiliar surroundings without a map — or rather, what is even more distressing: *with* a map but one that has become so frayed and torn that it now gives us only a terrifyingly incomplete, even distorted view of where we might really be.

However, I do not intend to produce a new map. I shall not seek to classify the European Parliament in terms of comparative government and politics or to resolve the ambivalence of its place in international relations. Instead I shall attempt to sketch a more pragmatic and constructive approach, which might make it easier, at least for practitioners, to live with the uncertainty and complexity and yet at the same time perceive actions they could usefully take to advance the cause of the European Parliament.

Unlike most political scientists, I do not assume that the European Parliament can be understood only as belonging either to a political 'system', even an embryonic one, or to an international 'system', even one facing serious transformation. Indeed, the way political scientists use the concept of system in both these contexts can be blamed for a lot that has gone astray in both the theory and the practice of 'European integration'. An awful lot of integration theory is tautological. As soon as one has fallen into the trap of assuming that the end of the process (or even more so the process itself) is an integrated (or integrating) system, in the sense of a harmonious, uniform whole, then anything and everything that serves the maintenance of the 'system' can be justified as 'integration'. Whether it is good or bad in its real or instantaneous effects becomes beside the point, and the fact that modern industrial society inevitably gives rise to social conflict is ignored or denied. Scholars and practitioners of European integration thus find themselves in a predicament similar to that caused by the emperor, famously mentioned by Borges, who commanded his subjects to produce a map of the empire so perfect that it covered exactly all of the territory, only to suffer the same fate as the empire itself, which went into irreparable decay since all its energy had gone into cartography.[2]

In other words, our problem in European integration (as in so much else in our present condition) is, less that we find ourselves with an unknown destination, than that we are trying to find our way by relying on a map that, like the fabled emperor's, is inevitably decayed, and by relying on this representation so exclusively that it has replaced for us the reality of where we are: *it is our ignorance of where we are now, at whatever point of the journey we may be, that is the actual problem*. The reference to Magritte in the title of the present chapter, or rather to Foucault's essay on Magritte, is, therefore, intended to highlight a general fault in the study — and increasingly also the practice — of European integration. As Baudrillard says: 'The territory no longer precedes the map, nor survives it. Henceforth it is the map that precedes the territory'.[3]

Since this is only a theoretical predicament, there is a way out of it. We do not need to get stuck with the problem of 'systems' and 'integration' (or cartography) in order to say something useful about the European Parliament. However, in order to find release from that theoretical predicament, it is necessary very much to take to heart Magritte's (and Foucault's) warning that the acts of labelling and classifying, or more generally *ordering*, can just as easily plunge us into the absurd as into the rational, where they are normally meant to lead. By comparing it to one of Magritte's famous pipes I am not trying to suggest facetiously that we should regard the European Parliament as some kind of amorphous surrealistic object floating in indefinite space — even though the building in Brussels especially designed for the Parliament may seem, ironically, to invite just such a description. Nor do I wish to embark, as so many social scientists nowadays do, trying to get in tune with the post-modern world they inhabit, on a celebration of ambivalence or a general invitation to share the inebriate delights of disorder.

On the contrary, I write from a strong preference in favour of order, from an enduring faith in reason as a source of practical as well as intellectual direction, from a persistently anxious concern that living with government is better than living without it, and from a conviction, severely tested by personal experience, that freedom is conditional on the disciplined observance of appropriate rules of conduct. In short, I am admitting the possibility, indeed the desirability, of an alternative order, one that the European Parliament has a necessary part in bringing into being, and that Parliament also needs for the sake of acquiring identity and purpose of its own.

At present any such new order is inchoate and exists at best only in ambivalence. The political structure of European Union unquestionably possesses both of those qualities. However, this condition neither can nor should be tolerated indefinitely, and it is certainly remediable. Two recent developments are coming to a head in such a way as to make some conclusion of the European Union's existential crisis inevitable: the commencement of currency union in 1999, and the deferrable but ultimately unavoidable further enlargement of membership to include central and eastern Europe.

The inability of diplomacy by the member states to provide the political guidance and discipline that is required to meet these two major current challenges is demonstrated by the recurrent experience of treaty revision as a method of reform, above all in the Treaty on European Union, signed at Maastricht in 1992, and in the Treaty of Amsterdam of 1997, which is expected to come into force during 1999 once it is ratified by the few remaining states that have not yet done so. In fact, the inter-governmental negotiations for the Amsterdam Treaty dodged the main issues of both Economic and Monetary Union (EMU) and further enlargement. The new treaty does make some reform of the Union's common institutions, mainly by increasing the powers of the European Parliament.[4] This has already raised expectations of an increased influence for members of the Parliament, who face new elections in June 1999. However, there is still no new constitutional settlement, and the role of the institutions is still founded on treaty provisions that are incomplete, highly ambiguous and even in some respects contradictory. From past experience, negotiations by the regular procedure to amend the existing treaties only add to these difficulties. The present institutions now face the daunting prospect of implementing the complexities added by Amsterdam and then preparing for yet another planned round of negotiations to coincide with the next enlargement of membership. However, that enlargement, if only in terms of the number of new member states that will need to be represented (possibly six to begin with followed shortly by another four, if not six or seven), has consequences that demand structural change, not just the usual horse-trading over additional placements and compensatory payments.

As a preliminary to a series of research papers on more specialised themes, this essay asks how the European Parliament might help to lead a way out of this confusion and crisis. Leaving others to collect and interpret the facts pertaining to the observations I make here, most of the latter will be analytical and hypothetical, encapsulated in the seven theorems signalled in the title. To the extent that I believe these state some simple and unavoidable truths about the real conditions in which the European Parliament does operate, I am suggesting them as a viable and relevant foundation for a new series of empirical and analytical studies.

Chapters 2, 3 and 4 present the results of a mainly philosophical reflection on the problem of identifying the problem we need to address, a task made more difficult by the massive growth in quantity and complexity of academic and other contributions to the debate on 'European integration' from various points of view and with all kinds of special pleading. I have tried to clear out the junk mail and that addressed to residents (or spouses) who have long since gone elsewhere, and to give priority to those bills that need to be paid immediately. As a result I find that integration, or the lack of it, might not be the real source of the problem and might not be its solution either. Only *ersatz* integration is attainable by political action alone, even under the happy circumstances of a secure government.

Nevertheless, the Union does not need, and ought not, to live in perpetual crisis and disorder, both of which cost all those involved an inexcusable waste of scarce resources. Chapters 5 and 6 develop my alternative thesis that the European Parliament exists not in order to promote 'political integration', nor for that matter only to provide a superficial legitimation for power that states have found it convenient to exercise supranationally, but rather as a response to genuine and justified unease at the human and social consequences of the decline of the nation-state, and the growing incapacity of existing political institutions, in the face both of transnational economic forces and of new threats to peace.

In short, I suggest that the realistic and pragmatic way to regard the purpose of the European Parliament in the next century is as an instrument of necessary social change. Although Parliament is by no means the only agency for this purpose, its success will depend on the extent to which a large majority of people of many nations in Europe, and also in the neighbouring regions, including both present and future member states of the Union, can feel the benefits of social cohesion and on that basis cultivate a sense of shared community. In chapter 5 I develop the hypothesis that a genuine European constituency of opinion, interest and identity already exists, and requires only a more effective channel of political representation to manifest itself. In chapter 6 I offer some preliminary observations as to how one might evaluate the Parliament's capacity to influence economic and social conditions by the use of public power. It should be a major task of future investigation to spell out the requirements of these two aims: the identification of a distinctively European sense of community; and the mobilisation of public power on its behalf.

These same aims are vital to the success of both EMU and the transition in central and eastern Europe, including the wider consequences of both for global welfare and security. Those two major impending issues invoke the supremely political task of defining boundaries. EMU implies a much stronger definition of the temporal boundary between the political and the administrative, between that which continues to be the subject-matter of transient deals and negotiations that trade in power and what in the common interest must be put beyond manipulation, settled by rules fixed over the long term, and entrusted to those without a personal stake in the outcome (in this case the management of credit and currency). The question of further enlargement is also acutely that of whether, and if so how, Europe can be defined, not only geographically or legally, but also socially and above all politically. The European Parliament has a central and unique contribution to defining borders in both these respects and the conclusions to this study in chapter 7 indicate possible lines of research into what that role might be.

2. The Anarchical Union

The starting point of any serious study of the European Parliament as a political institution must be the presumption that, unlike any institution in previous experience with which its name invites comparison, this 'parliament' does not operate as part of, or in relation to, a system of government. As three noted commentators say: 'The Parliament operates within the framework of a set of institutions ... which have no exact counterparts in national political systems'.[5] The same authors also point out that the European Parliament can, on the other hand, be no more usefully compared with the assemblies sometimes included in international organisations, like the Assembly of the Council of Europe.

My first theorem states this simple, almost self-evident presumption:

THEOREM 1 *THE EUROPEAN PARLIAMENT'S ROLE IS AMBIVALENT AND INDEFINABLE TO THE EXTENT THAT IT DOES NOT BELONG TO A TYPICAL NATIONAL OR INTERNATIONAL SYSTEM.*

The implications of this theorem for the present study are, nevertheless, disturbing, since I have already questioned the validity of understanding European integration either as a process of constructing a political system or as a specific, if deviant, model new to the international system. The question is whether this leaves us with no alternative but to treat the role of this institution as hopelessly ambivalent and vague.

The term 'ambivalent' is used here and elsewhere in this study in the sense given by Zigmunt Bauman:

'Ambivalence, the possibility of assigning an object or an event to more than one category, is a language-specific disorder: a failure of the naming (segregating) function that language is meant to perform. The main symptom of disorder is the acute discomfort we feel when we are unable to read the situation properly and to choose between alternative actions.'[6]

In fact, as Bauman is at pains to explain, ambivalence in this sense is very much a modern, or rather post-modern, condition. It is itself a product of the modernising need to classify and categorise, while it is the very urgency of this process characteristic of social as well as natural science that causes the proliferation and abundance of ambivalence in all aspects of our present world.

Indeed, it is in this sense that the real problem in both study and practice of European integration is the desire to identify a 'political system' to which such an institution can be classified. It was during the 1960s that the relatively few (and mostly American) political scientists then interested in the European Economic Community (EEC) began to treat it *ex hypothesi* as a political system or 'polity' in its own right, if only in embryo.[7] In Europe this development was welcomed as enlarging the dimensions of academic study of European integration, which had been confined largely to international relations, law and economics. The European Community was in fact the product of aspirations to create more than just another international organisation, and it had serious political consequences capable of undermining well-established ideas and theories. This did not, however, provide sufficient reason to assume that the Community's primary purpose was to establish a political system, comparable to those already classified by comparative political science.

The way the concept of integration was used by those who wanted to treat the Community as a 'would-be polity' seems to have been very much influenced by sociological theories recommending the analysis of social, and by derivation also political, action as inherently belonging to a self-regulating system. Political scientists especially thus came to regard 'European integration' almost unthinkingly as referring to the construction of a new supranational political system, if not state. This is not the place to pursue scholastic issues of that kind, but in fact this particular malapropism with integration has had very serious and enduring effects on practice. It has given a kind of scientific legitimation to those engaged in politics to treat the whole issue of 'European integration' as concerning support for or opposition to the creation of a new super-state.

Although the common habit of describing European Union as a 'system' or 'polity' may betray no more than an innocent desire to be idiomatic, such careless thinking can all too easily turn idiom into analogy.[8] To try to classify the European Parliament in terms of comparative politics, as if it did belong to an established system of government, is actually to perpetrate ambiguity, not to resolve it. Parliaments are conventionally treated in comparative politics as being functional to the maintenance of a political system. Michael Mezey says:

> 'Functionalism provides the terminology most frequently employed by political scientists in discussions of the legislature as an independent variable. Such analyses begin by asking what functions the legislature performs for the larger political system in which it operates. The answers to such enquiries have been grouped into three broad categories: policy-making, representation and legitimization.'[9]

The leading British authority on parliamentary studies found that an earlier typology of Mezey's was empirically justified by a comparison of several European parliaments, the main differences in performance, behaviour and public appreciation being explicable by 'cultural factors'. Philip Norton thus arrived at the extraordinarily complacent conclusion that: 'Legislatures in Western Europe appear to have consequences for their political systems (*sic*) which have usually been borne out of, and continue to satisfy, national expectations and values'.[10] To treat parliaments as functional to a self-regulating political system can have strange results even when applied to a nation-state with a government. When applied to something like European Union the possibilities of confusion are almost endless. Moreover, since the European Parliament would rightly claim a part in the very construction of any new political order at European level, to regard it as merely functional to such a 'system' must be absurd (except in so far as it makes sense to regard the mother as functional to the child, the artist to the picture).

The temptation to corrupt idiom by analogy is still forgivable to the extent that the original European project of economic or functional 'integration' was itself highly ambiguous. The supranational institutions themselves, the European Parliament in particular, along with most of the member states' governments have always assumed that there was an overriding political mission. The European Community was to some extent a reincarnation of earlier postwar projects of political union that had more or less failed. The famous declaration by French foreign minister, Robert Schuman, of 9 May 1950, launching the successful initial project for a Coal and Steel Community, described the ultimate goal as 'federation'. A reasonably circumstantial draft treaty for a European political union was actually considered by ministers of the original Six following their signature of a subsequent treaty to establish a European Defence Community in 1952. This text, formulated by a special committee of the assembly of the new Community, amounted to a draft federal constitution, but it was abandoned when the defence treaty itself was rejected by the French National Assembly in the summer of 1954.

After this setback, the more pragmatic or 'functionalist' approach, concentrating on economic 'integration' rather than matters considered vital to state sovereignty like defence or the construction of new political institutions, seemed the only way forward for those who sought an alternative to the methods of conventional international diplomacy for establishing a new order of peace and economic recovery in western Europe. The two Rome treaties establishing the EEC and Euratom provided for common institutions with some supranational powers like those of the High Authority of the ECSC (though the term 'supranational' itself was dropped). However, although retrospectively it became orthodox legal opinion to regard these institutions as operating within a distinct and autonomous constitutional framework, this was much weaker than anything the federalists had earlier proposed.

What the Community treaties provided was, in effect, no more than a method — the *community method* — which consisted of a proposal to transform the economic relations between the states concerned into a 'common market', by means of a progressive transfer of powers to common institutions (eventually designated as European Parliament, Council, Commission and Court of Justice) over a period of time that was not in every respect fixed in advance. Nevertheless, the EEC treaty declared itself 'concluded for an unlimited period' (Article 240). The Court of Justice succeeded in entrenching the doctrine that the process of establishing a common market as the basis of an 'ever closer union', inaugurated by that treaty, was both irreversible and evolutionary, or progressive, that is, liable to be complemented by new provisions added at a later date. The treaty endowed the common institutions with what amounted to legislative power (especially under Articles 100 and 235) and included a due procedure for its own amendment (in Article 236). It also explicitly provided that other European states could become members by submitting applications for acceptance according to a special procedure.

A total of nine states have of course so far acceded to membership using this procedure at different times over the past twenty-five years.

Each of the new members has accepted the established corpus of legally-binding provisions, either contained in the founding treaties themselves or made subsequently in accordance with them (the *acquis communautaire*) up to the date of its entry, and the enlargement of membership has so far required only minor amendments to the founding treaties. Until 1986 these had not been subject to major amendment for any reason. In that year the Single European Act was adopted, following a series of varied proposals for at last transforming the Community into a political union.

The only one of these proposals that was substantial and coherent was, in fact, the Draft Treaty on European Union adopted by the European Parliament on its own initiative in 1984. This amounted to another fully-fledged draft constitution, even more detailed and comprehensive than that produced by the former 'ad hoc assembly' of 1952. This document went much further than the member states were able to do with the unanimity required, either legally to amend the founding treaties, or practically to give the community method a constitutional basis that would prove at all effective. All the state governments were able to agree were regular joint declarations committing themselves to 'political union' at some later date. These were usually grandiloquent but never credible. Indeed, the best the governments could do in the ironically named *Single* Act was to fudge the whole issue even more by engaging in what was essentially not a single but a double act, which took two quite contrary steps: in one part, the states wrote into the EEC treaty a number of new provisions for expanding the functions and powers of the existing institutions that had already been on the Community's agenda for some time; however, in another part, they formalised their own existing intergovernmental procedures of European Political Cooperation as a separate continuing activity, thus implicitly rejecting proposals for political union.

The Maastricht Treaty on European Union only compounded this ambiguity. Some may have hoped that the transition to Union from Community would bring a long overdue constitutional and political settlement, and put it beyond equivocation that the common institutions of Parliament, Council, Commission and Court constituted, in effect, a federal government. On the contrary, Maastricht represented a messy compromise between, on the one hand, this more orthodox view, often now typified as 'federalist', and an altogether contrary understanding of 'integration'. Indeed, two member states, Denmark and the United Kingdom, vetoed the very use of the word 'federal' in any formal text. Such an 'anti-federalist' view had been gaining ground all the time since the inauguration of the Community method almost forty years previously.

Roughly speaking, the 'anti-federalist' doctrine, most vociferous in the national positions adopted by Denmark and the UK, but influential to some extent in most member states and especially in France (most overtly among the past and present disciples of Charles de Gaulle), aspires to little more than a common space in which states that so choose conduct their relations with each other and collectively with third parties in accordance with an extensive mutual compact. The compact includes provision for common agencies (which may be legally designated as 'institutions' but do not warrant this appellation in fact) vested with a certain corpus of regulatory powers, for mainly economic objectives. These powers are treated by the contracting states by mutual consent as directly binding within their own legal systems. In other words, according to this heterodox but increasingly pervasive view of integration, the order inherited from the Community by the European Union should not be considered as deviating crucially from normal international relations. Integration might thus be defined as little more in effect than a permanent delegation of authority from a group of closely associated sovereign states to an 'international regime' (in so far as such an act can be permanent in any meaningful sense).[11]

Although the European Union of Maastricht does not replace the Community, except to supersede it in name, and actually extends the previous constitutional framework to provide for an economic and monetary union, it nevertheless sets out to undermine the irreversible and evolutionary character of the Community method, and marks out significant spheres of 'integration' that the states deliberately reserve for themselves.

The two spheres delineated in this way at Maastricht were, of course, the two 'pillars' of *common foreign and security policy* and *cooperation in justice and home affairs*. The common institutions were not wholly excluded from these spheres and were even given some new functions, but they were also made subordinate to the political authority of the states, exercised through the active and constant assertion of the role of member state governments (especially through the European Council, which is given some quasi-institutional functions by the Treaty on European Union). In this respect the ambiguity of Maastricht is palpable. Two quite different orders of legal authority are juxtaposed under the same roof of 'integration': respectively, quasi-federal relations in the Community sphere, or first pillar, and something much more akin to conventional international relations in the second and third pillars. The 1997 Treaty of Amsterdam explicitly confirms this polarity (Article 5) while declining to give the Union ('established' according to Article A of Maastricht) either unequivocal existence or legal personality.

These arrangements, however, only set the seal on the previous anarchical tendency of member states to enlarge their collective use of power on the authority of their own individual sovereignties, and without the need to obtain any kind of domestic constitutional authorisation — or even, before 1986, a formal treaty. Since it is impossible in practice, at least for purposes of efficient administration, to segregate areas of public policy from each other, inevitably the more member state governments sought to fill the spheres left vacant by the founding Community treaties, and developed their own special procedures and mechanisms for making common decisions within those spheres, the less it was feasible for the common institutions to exercise their own autonomous powers except in deference to the 'political will' of states' governments. When this will had not been already pronounced, or had been expressed only with equivocation, the Community institutions soon acquired the habit of seeking authorisation or clarification anew on their own initiative. When the obscurity of the pronounced directives of the governments arose from an actual or potential conflict with what the institutions thought was necessary under Community law, the same recourse to the same ultimate source of political authority nevertheless tended to occur.

In 1974 this heterodox but increasingly customary method of 'intergovernmentalism' was endowed with a certain formality and permanence, when the governments agreed to turn their own occasional extra-mural gatherings, previously called 'summit conferences' because they included the heads of each government, into the infelicitously named European Council. The name invites confusion with, on the one hand, the Council, which is one of the Community's common institutions, and, on the other hand, the Council of Europe, which is a relatively innocuous international organisation concerned mainly with human rights and cultural matters.[12] This body has subsequently operated on a regular basis as the apex of a series of inferior committees, meeting much more frequently, composed of foreign ministers or of diplomats, and has assumed, often by default, the standard functions of political direction, including those that belonged initially to the Commission or Council of the Community. Indeed, the common institutions have for some time now regularly looked to it for general guidance (and in some respects are now legally obliged to do so). Effectively, therefore, it is no longer only the Court of Justice that may give authentic interpretations of the common interest in terms of the founding treaties. In this respect anarchy has certainly replaced order, at least consitutional order.

The European Council has also become indispensable for resolving major disputes between the state governments, in this too supplanting one of the Commission's original main functions. Initially under the system of European Political Cooperation, the states also used the European Council, under the guise of approximating their own foreign policies, to take back responsibility for the mainly economic external relations transferred by the founding treaties to the common institutions, as well as to reassert generally the supremacy of foreign policy, and foreign ministries, in European affairs.

This special extension of national diplomacy, more subtle and complex in its origins, motivation and operation than any comparable procedure of international relations, really came into its own following the Franco-German initiative taken in the spring of 1990 for a new treaty of political union, which led two years later to Maastricht. Subsequently much of the typical activity of the state governments in European Council has been carried on even more intensively by the new readiness to make use of the procedures for amending the community treaties and establishing new treaty provisions, as in the protracted negotiations leading to Maastricht and Amsterdam, with the deleterious consequences for good administration already described earlier in this chapter. The Union is therefore governed, if at all, by a kind of standing diplomatic conference, assisted by supranational institutions, but ultimately unanswerable, except in so far as each member of the conference is accountable to his or her own government. If this is government, then it can be compared with the government of any recognised political system or state only very approximately.

The Community method, while for reasons already given here itself substituted in some respects for a genuine government, nevertheless had a constitutional foundation in the treaties that has been upheld by judicial authority throughout the member states. The Community was moreover obliged to perform tasks and achieve objectives of public policy that certainly demand characteristics pertaining to good government in any modern state. Since it has remained in the interests of all member states that the functions of the Community be well administered, why then has anarchy come to prevail? There are various possible explanations. Perhaps too many influential people found these original aspirations of the rule of law and constitutionalism less attractive or convenient than the alternative. Some have taken up the thesis that even the objectives of the founding treaties could be reached efficiently only by increasingly pragmatic resort to 'intergovernmentalism'.[13] The Community method could have simply failed through lack of skill or effort in its own application. For my own thesis concerning the European Parliament, it will be enough here to concentrate on one particular aspect of the distraint, renunciation or miscarriage — whichever it was — that deprived the Community method of its original promise and Europe of the good administration its people doubtless deserve.

3. The Democratic Deficit

Resistance to the development of federal institutions in Europe, including the European Parliament, is often grounded in fear that it would lead to under-representation of the great diversity of interests and opinions currently protected and facilitated by the pluralistic democracy within the nation-states. The rulers of states have themselves sometimes exploited such concerns to further their own anti-federalism. Nevertheless, intergovernmentalism undoubtedly gained at the expense of federalism partly on account of the inability of the European Community and its apologists to meet this challenge, which has now become almost notorious as the 'democratic deficit'.

In fact, the cause of the democratic deficit is not federalism, if only because federalism has been too weak an element in the construction of European Union to be the cause of anything significant. Federalists have always been relentless and vociferous in their criticism of the European Community's shortcomings in terms of democracy. If any doctrine or theory can be blamed for such a practical deficiency, the experience of European integration since 1945 would suggest that failure to attend to the needs of democracy may be a major shortcoming of a tendency to rely too much on the conventional methods of diplomacy and international relations.

The 'democratic deficit' seems to have been introduced into the discourse of European integration by the then Belgian prime minister, Leo Tindemans, in his famous report made to the European Council in 1974. This was the first of a series of initiatives to revive the project of political union, and restore it as the main objective of the community method. In this original usage the term referred to the effects on parliaments, and indeed other representative institutions, within member states of the progressive transfer of legislative power to supranational institutions as a consequence of the EEC treaty. The typically federalist inference from this was that integration required the development of alternative forms of representation at a European level. The reference to democracy in the Tindemans report could be seen from this point of view, which was supported by a majority of the nine member states at that time, to give greater urgency to the case for introducing direct elections to the European Parliament and increasing its powers. In fact, the states did shortly afterwards unanimously agree to implement at least partially the treaty provisions for direct elections.[14] Moreover, Parliament's own demands for greater recognition proved to be increasingly influential, while its recently enlarged budgetary powers were also about to come into effect (see also chapter 6 below).

However, while some (including Tindemans himself) saw the problem of democracy as providing a strong reason for constructing more federal institutions, to others it was a no less strong reason for resisting any such development, and for them the Tindemans report itself was probably a delaying tactic. Consequently, contrary to the federalist intention, the democratic deficit became a convenient rationalisation for the general tendency of member state governments to assert more influence in the affairs of the Community's institutions, to reserve to themselves collective decisions on many matters that might otherwise have become additions to the responsibility of the supranational institutions, and even implicitly to reclaim powers that had already been transferred. This helps to explain the development of the European Council. It may also explain the recently increased willingness to resort to treaty amendment, since national parliaments apparently obtain a more direct participation in so far as the amending treaties have to be ratified by each member state according to its own consititutional requirements (which usually do include express parliamentary approval of the full text, and may also include approval by a national referendum).

In fact, these reasons are all spurious, factually unfounded and even in the case of some states scandalously hypocritical. This particular argument in favour of intergovernmentalism needs to be turned on its head:

THEOREM 2 *THE POWERS OF NATIONAL PARLIAMENTS IN RELATION TO THE EUROPEAN UNION IS A FUNCTION PRIMARILY OF THE CONSTITUTIONAL AND POLITICAL CONDITIONS PREVAILING WITHIN EACH STATE.*

In other words, whether, and how much, parliaments (or other nationally representative institutions) are able to influence and control what is done in the name of European integration depends most of all on what they are permitted and empowered to do *by their own states*. A further, more suggestive proposition is associated with this second theorem:

THEOREM 3 *THE PRACTICE OF DEMOCRACY BY THE MEMBER STATES IS A NECESSARY CONDITION OF ITS PRACTICE BY THE EUROPEAN UNION.*

If we are concerned about any threat to democracy in the European Union, then we should look primarily for the cause, and also for a possible remedy, to the constitutional and political conditions prevailing in each member state.

Indeed, the treaties establishing the European Communities left the member states' own institutions intact. They contained nothing expressly intended or designed to prevent national parliaments, or any other representative bodies within states, from continuing to exercise their normal functions. There is not even mention of member state parliaments as such, negatively or positively, except with respect to the transitional provisions for appointing the members of the European Parliament, or 'Assembly' as it was then called, initially composed of delegations from state parliaments.[15] Not only was this institution, therefore, liable to be overruled in almost every respect, except its own internal procedure and organisation, by decision of the representatives of the member states in the Council but it was also very much itself a creature of parliamentary politics within the member states.

Although the institutions of the Community could claim authority from the treaties to adopt legally-binding enactments without first consulting, or even informing, parliaments within the member states, the authority extended for the most part to a kind of legal instrument that would not as a rule occupy parliaments directly or habitually. Those enactments were for the most part of a type and substance (at first to do mainly with international trade) that would normally in a state be left to the public administration, in the form of secondary or 'delegated' legislation.

Even so, the power to adopt *regulations, directives,* and *decisions* (in accordance with Article 189 of the EEC treaty) was rarely entrusted to the Commission acting on its own authority. Most often it required full and express endorsement by the Council, acting on a proposal of the

Commission, and always did so whenever the issue concerned was likely to affect the interests of a sizeable group of producers or traders, or raise important matters of public policy, such as public expenditure or existing general legislation within any state.

Since it was composed of representatives nominated by the 'governments' of member states, the Council might for that very reason be assumed to represent also the parliaments of states. The governments of member states used different arrangements to keep national parliaments abreast of the regulatory activity of the common institutions; in many cases they seem to have done very little. Nevertheless, the various arrangements seem to have worked without major upset in most cases for most of the time, especially before the first enlargement of membership in 1973. This may be because most of the original six member states had become accustomed, since the postwar settlement at least, to enjoy a high degree of political consensus in their domestic affairs, being normally governed by wide-ranging coalitions of different political parties, used to sharing power with each other, and capable of managing effectively (by no means all the time but for a remarkably large amount of it) the social divisions of late industrial capitalism. The main exception to this pattern was of course France, which since 1958 (coincidentally the year when the EEC treaty came into effect) was governed by a semi-presidential regime, in which the role of parliament was deliberately restricted and for that very reason not likely to be a major issue of conflict in European affairs (though other issues were).[16]

On the other hand, the effects on parliament became a central issue in British politics during the run-up to accession and also the subsequent 're-negotiation' in 1975, and also gained prominence in Denmark during the same period. Perhaps one reason why the parliamentary aspect of European integration was so much emphasised in political agonising over membership in these states, and consequently became a major problem not only for them on a continuing basis but for others too, was the very lack of consensus on the issue of membership itself, which was a cause of schism within the governing party in both the UK and Denmark. Another interesting hypothesis is that both these states may have had special difficulty in keeping engagements entered into by treaty, since both their governments at the relevant times lacked the support of a majority of the electorate. Indeed, minority government (in terms of electoral support in the UK and parliamentary support in

Denmark) has tended to be the rule rather than the exception in both these states, as have sharp intra-party divisions on European policy.

Tindemans and others may have emphasised the issue of democracy at this time partly out of a good-natured effort to appease these reluctant new members, though both had other reasons of more material national interest to remain obstructive. Following major political changes that eventually turned out to favour the restoration of parliamentary democracy, Greece, Portugal and Spain all became serious candidates for membership during the 1970s and the Community was thus to some extent obliged at least to pretend to have a benign effect on democracy in order to encourage them. However, the previous dictatorships in those countries had been tolerated by Community members in the North Atlantic Alliance and had not been disqualified from associate status with the Community. There were, in fact, a number of structural reasons why the European Community needed seriously to address the issue of its own democratic deficit at this time.

One of these reasons was the increasing powers of the supranational institutions themselves, and the growing demand for even further transfers to them of the use of public power. By the 1970s the member states, whether acting through the institutions or using ad hoc intergovernmental procedures, were actively planning an economic and monetary union, and implementing or expanding provisions for using public finance to pursue objectives of common policy, in particular, what are now known as the structural funds. This type of instrument became all the more politically significant by the approval in 1970 of a system of 'own resources' to finance expenditure from the Community's budget (in accordance with Article 200 EEC). The system came into effect in 1975.

In addition, especially during the 1980s, the member states' governments became increasingly willing to accept votes in Council by qualified majority, as and when provided by the treaties. The Single Act significantly extended the provisions subject to majority voting by Council, especially for the purpose of speeding implementation of the programme of measures to complete the internal market by 1992. Of course, when Council did adopt decisions by majority, there was even less than usual that parliaments in states in the minority could do about it. Some might also have regretted the consequent decline in national parliaments' capacity to insist on the use of a 'veto' by their ministerial representatives in Council.

On the other hand, Council's willingness to resort to majority votes to adopt specific measures, proposed in accordance with a programme of economic and social improvements approved in advance unanimously by national governments, ought to have been seen as a way of reducing the democratic deficit. Since national parliaments had already, if only implicitly, approved those decisions, by supporting the governments that made them, they could hardly complain if the Council proceeded to implement them as expeditiously as possible. It is interesting that a veto should have been regarded a necessary safeguard of democracy. That it should implies that the parliaments concerned cannot have had very much confidence in their own ministers. Why were the national parliaments that were most aggrieved so ill-informed and suspicious about what their own ministers were trying to achieve through their participation in Council? How had those parliaments come to approve their own states' accession to the Community, when they so much feared and disliked the consequences?

Indeed, the effects on democracy of previous participation by governments in normal international relations were not propitious. Membership of Nato, for example, restricts the power of its member states' parliaments to influence and control policy for national defence, including public expenditure, while there have been occasions when even west European governments have been obliged to adjust their economic policies against parliamentary opinion in order to conform to the IMF's rules of 'conditionality'. Less organised forms of international cooperation, such as the G7 meetings of major OECD member states, and even the actions of private corporations operating transnationally, present national institutions with conditions over which they have little or no control.[17]

There can be little doubt that the democratic deficit that has grown to become a major issue of European integration is no more than symptomatic of a much wider and more persistent challenge to democracy arising from the increased involvement of governments in international relations, increased both relative to their previous degree of involvement, and also in terms of the nature and number of responsibilities devolved on governments, or assumed by them, as a consequence. The growing resort in European integration to methods of international relations rather than the orthodox community method may be seen as an extension of that same trend, and therefore as only exacerbating the problem.

However, another reason why democracy became a growing issue in the Community was that the general public grew to be far less satisfied with what the Community method seemed able to achieve materially than had been the case in the 1960s, particularly with respect to the level of employment and the growth in real incomes of those already employed. To this extent, it is also necessary to ask how much effective difference this pressure of opinion made to the actions of governments in the process of European integration, more particularly in their determination of policy with respect to economic affairs. The increased involvement of national governments, and devolution of power to them, does not seem to have made people any more contented with the outcome. Certainly, the evidence of public dissatisfaction following the Maastricht treaty, and the failure of at least three states to ratify that treaty with more than the barest minimum of popular approval, did not say much for intergovernmentalism, on the counts either of democracy or of efficiency. The search for a more attractive alternative leads us back into some more basic, and classical, thoughts about democratic government.

4. For And Against Constitutional Union

All modern states, however much they may set out to practise democracy, are to some extent prevented from doing so by their involvement in international relations. The practice of democracy within states is no guarantee of its practice in international society, nor that the benefits of peace and prosperity will be equitably distributed between nations. Indeed, one of the effects of democracy within states might be to encourage them to act more selfishly, and with a more fervent attachment to national interest.[18]

From these observations we may derive a fourth theorem, which gives a simple explanation why the European Parliament exists at all:

THEOREM 4 *THE PRACTICE OF DEMOCRACY IN EACH MEMBER STATE IS NOT A SUFFICIENT CONDITION OF ITS PRACTICE IN THE EUROPEAN UNION.*

In other words, the argument that peace and welfare can never be adequately guaranteed until some form of democracy has been somehow constructed internationally applies *a fortiori* to European integration, which aims to involve supranational authorities in an exceptionally wide and detailed manner in the ordinary affairs of the citizens of its member states. We may conjecture that the more national governments assume the power to determine the policy of European Union and its execution, the worse will be the consequences for democracy. In order to appreciate the full weight of this deduction, we need to take account of another theorem:

THEOREM 5 *THE PRACTICE OF DEMOCRACY AT THE LEVEL OF THE EUROPEAN UNION IS A NECESSARY CONDITION OF ITS PRACTICE WITHIN THE MEMBER STATES.*

This, of course, amounts to an inversion of Theorem 3 — that its practice by the member states is a necessary condition of the practice of democracy by the Union. It follows also that the European Parliament is not necessarily in opposition to national parliaments within the member state. Its own acquisition of power is not equivalent to a corresponding loss of power by national parliaments, though the power of the federal parliament may be contrary to that of national parliaments in certain respects, in so far as they could not exercise the same power in the same instance without the risk of contradiction. The two levels are not, however, opposites, and more often than not can be complementary. They each have a role, albeit usually a distinct and separate one, in ensuring that European integration is as favourable as possible, and as little damaging as possible, to democratic values.

Theorems 4 and 5 amount to a recognition that national sovereignty is no longer an efficient means of ensuring democracy. Although now more widely accepted by students of international relations, such a suggestion is still highly disputable, and prone to be disputed by states themselves as well as by all exponents of nationalism as a political ideology. It challenges two basic tenets of nationalism that have been associated historically: the conviction that a viable and genuine sense of political community is feasible only on the national principle, be this applied in an economic, cultural or even ethnic sense; and the theory that the civil rights and freedoms enjoyed by those fortunate enough to be citizens of a nation-state, including democratic institutions where they exist, depend essentially on the principle of state sovereignty.

This nationalist fundamentalism seems to have enjoyed a recent revival and especially as a reaction to the demise of communism in Eastern Europe, though it was always present in the west, especially in the larger and former imperial nation-states, as a countervailing, and almost now prevailing, force against the Community method and certainly against the development of its federal elements. Its two leading exponents have been Charles de Gaulle and Margaret Thatcher.

Against nationalism run two main currents of thought, which have been implicit or latent not only in the process of European integration itself but also in a more broadly cosmopolitan and internationalist movement, of which functionalism may be considered an earlier version. These correspond to the two nationalist tenets. One is the view that there not only can be, but is, such a thing as a people common to different states, even nation-states, and capable of forming a political entity, indeed a *community* generating its own values, interests, shared hopes and fears, and even objectives of public policy. The other is a concern, obversely to Theorem 2, that state sovereignty is as capable of justifying and tolerating tyranny as it is freedom, and that only the extension of constitutional principles and methods beyond the nation-state can adequately safeguard civic values either within the boundaries of states or beyond them.

Both these currents, and especially the second, are familiar enough to students of political thought as having been influenced primarily by the work of the eighteenth century philosopher Immanuel Kant. Exponents of such ideas today would hardly if ever refer to it, but they are also closely associated with the more practical discourse of federalism, as this has evolved from Kant's own time to the present day. Nevertheless, federalism, if only on account of its very pragmatism, is subject to a great variety of interpretations and has been observed in such diverse applications, that it has become extremely difficult to identify one coherent set of principles or guides to practice as uniquely Federalist.[19] Indeed, the terms 'federal' and 'federation' now have so many varied connotations, that they can hardly be mentioned in ordinary public debate about European integration without arousing all kinds of prejudicial opinions.

Above all, there is the widespread misconception that federalism inevitably intends, or at least implies, the formation of a composite 'federal' state. Certainly a distinction needs to be made in political analysis between: on the one hand, 'federations' as present or past examples of political entities founded on federal principles, but which have normally turned out in practice to be identical for most purposes, especially those of international relations, with sovereign states; and on the other hand, 'federalism' as a diverse corpus of political thought sharing certain common principles and generally inclined towards pragmatism.[20]

The confusion and distortion of federalism in the present discourse of European Union probably owe much to the way the federalist idea is so closely associated in practice with a particular case of federation, that of the American union. This turned out in fact to be a constitutional and political experiment that was nationalist as much as federalist in inspiration, and it is surely not too historicist to assume that under the prevailing circumstances it had to be the nationalist tendencies that prevailed.[21] The USA thus became a paradigm case of national integration, and perhaps the most extraordinary assertion of the national principle, in view of the cultural and ethnic diversity of the society (even compared with Germany). Nevertheless, in searching for a solution to the current predicament of European states, obliged to work with a very imperfect confederation, it is difficult to avoid re-visiting the case of the so-called 'federalists' who assisted the American states facing a similar predicament towards the end the eighteenth century.

James Madison, in particular, then argued in favour of endowing the proposed union with its own political institutions which should be capable of acting independently of the states in certain crucial respects, not only with respect to common defence, which was normally the primary and often unique function of any initial act of federation or confederation. Madison, like the other American federalists, was driven to this conclusion by the pragmatic consideration that the existing confederation allowed only for government that was endemically indecisive, incoherent, corruptible and short-sighted. He took this view not only because of the needs of the American people for defence against their actual and potential enemies, but also no less importantly because of the remarkable opportunities for economic and social development that the American people had the potential to enjoy.

Madison, possibly more than the other federalists, was also strongly influenced by political ideas. The principal threat to the republican and democratic values that had in principle at least inspired the American revolution was in Madison's view a 'tyranny of the majority' within the states themselves. He saw this danger primarily in the effects of 'faction', meaning not only political partisanship (as in its later more common meaning), but also the organisation of sectional economic interests, as well as the attachment to, and propagation of, religious or other beliefs held by particular groups. To avoid oppression by majorities in the states was a necessary condition, in other words, of republican pluralism, including genuine freedom of political association, economic competition and freedom of belief and expression. The only effective way of guaranteeing this condition was to provide for a common government with its own legislative, executive and judicial power over and above the states. However, the fundamental inspiration of this federal government was to be the people themselves, who would also be both the ultimate source of arbitration between it and the governments of the several constituent states, and the ultimate guarantor of the federal government's respect for diversity, freedom and justice.

The conservative defenders of state sovereignty in Europe today seem to have much in common with their American counterparts who opposed the new 'federal' constitution in 1778 and against whom Madison's arguments were mainly deployed. The 'anti-federalists' of that time and place also used political ideas to justify their own preference for a much looser kind of confederal union, making much in particular of Montesquieu's claims on behalf of the greater stability and security afforded by a more balanced form of government. Montesquieu's preferred system was also described as federal, but its advantages for personal liberty as well as for social cohesion depended on the maintenance of a balance or equilibrium between different powers, none of which could claim to be literally sovereign over the others. Similarly beneficial effects are expected to flow from equilibrium, or at least equivalence, between sovereign states in the theory of balance of power so crucial to classical international relations.[22]

Montesquieu's version of confederation, indeed, seems to be revived in the 'liberal intergovernmentalism' or 'cooperative federalism' recently expounded by some academic apologists of European Union. Samuel Beer's paraphrase of how the early American anti-federalists viewed the practical advantages of Montesquieu's 'confederate republic' certainly evokes the conservative model of European Union that the British and Danes have done so much to impose on the rest of us:

> 'The representatives of the member states at the center will be like ambassadors of independent nations, and their discussion and decision-making will have the nature of diplomatic bargaining and balancing among the interests of their constituencies. An ambassador is a delegate: his task is to take the national interest of his country as given and to promote this end by the most effective means at his disposal. Similarly, in a republic on the confederate model, the various members would have their several internally determined interests which the general framework of government would defend, but not invade, regulate or modify. The members of the confederation could bargain over the exchange of benefits that that would be useful to their respective purposes ... In this process, as in rational choice theory, the preferences of the parties would remain unchanged.'[23]

A similar model seems to be implied by Alan Milward's thesis that the Community method was relatively successful, not because it achieved the bare removal of economic borders, let alone the re-making of political systems, but because it enabled existing states to maintain social cohesion internally.[24]

However, what seems to have appealed to the American anti-federalists above all was Montesquieu's assumption that government would be closest to the people, most reflective of their true wishes, as well as more stable and coherent in relatively small states. And the reason given for this preference was the theory that political rule was more likely to retain these virtues the more compact and homogeneous the society. In this respect the defenders of the sovereignty of the American states were to a large degree, like Montesquieu, inclined to a conservative view of political and social development, to the agrarian rather than the manufacturing interest, and less convinced of the advantages of modern ideas of democracy, industrialisation and freedom of trade. They were not, on the whole, modernisers or more particularly nationalists.

It is not only the comparison with Montesquieu's small republic that tends to make Milward's celebration of the welfare states of Western Europe appear outdated, if not nostalgic. In fact, the Community method has not been enough to save the European welfare state, which has been transformed over the past two decades in ways that foster neither the cohesion of national communities, nor the amelioration of social inequality. The deregulation of economic activity, the privatisation of many essential public services, the reduction, if not elimination, of budget deficits despite high levels of unemployment, and the increased flexibility of labour markets, have all been inspired by an ardent individualism rather than any genuinely communitarian philosophy. Moreover, they have tended to make those dependent on employment for a livelihood even more economically insecure, exposed to a degraded environment and culturally deprived. All European states seem to face a similar threat, different only in degree, to the social fabric of community, whether the main cause is seen as excessive migration, unemployment or other forms of social exclusion, the decline of primary social units such as the family, or the deterioration of public services.

This comparison between the conservative anti-federalists in the eighteenth century American confederation and their counterparts in European Union today highlights, therefore, a remarkable paradox, if not complete contradiction, in the assertion of nationalism in present conditions to defend democracy, or at least the sense of community on which it may be assumed to depend. The current anti-federalists in Europe would hardly want to be identified with a doctrine of collectivism, traditionalism and provincialism. However, this would seem to be the main historical, and possibly also theoretical, association of their own version of 'nationalism', which in the ideology that inspired the American union (and the later unions of Great Britain, Germany and Italy) was by contrast essentially individualist, modernist, and (initially at least) cosmopolitan.

The lineal descendant of that enlightened humanitarianism (in its historically previous version associated with a nationalism crucially different from what is mainly propounded or practised by that name in Europe today) is the federal or 'supranational' persuasion that has inspired the European Community method and sought to cultivate a new form of democracy by means of common institutions. The most learned, and indeed venerable teacher in this lineage now is Joseph Weiler, whose work transmits in essence the Madisonian principles in a European context:

> '... in the curtailment of the totalistic claim of the nation-state and the reduction of nationality as the principal referent for human intercourse, the community ideal of supranationalism is evocative of, and resonates with, Enlightenment ideas, with the privileging of the individual, with a different aspect of liberalism which has its progeny today in liberal notions of human rights. In this respect the community ideal is heir to Enlightenment liberalism. Supranationalism assumes a new, additional meaning which refers not to the relations among nations but to the ability of the individual to rise above his or her national closet.'[25]

The main issue for contemporary Europe is, therefore, not only federalism, but also *constitutionalism*.[26] How can the benefits of government, practised in accordance with the rule of law and democracy, be secured in a community that is too vague in terms of both territorial and social boundaries to be viable or even conceivable as a *nation*? How can I enjoy the virtues of being a citizen, and the necessary accompanying protection of a constitution, without a *sovereign*, and without all the yearning for differentiation, unequivocality, majesty and elevation from which that essentially androcentric concept is derived?[27]

5. The European Constituency: Interests, Movements, Issues

The revival of nationalism demonstrates that constitutional rules and procedures are not sufficient to provide for government that is acceptable in terms of democracy. Filling the democratic deficit of European Union is not only a matter of formulating the right treaty provisions and mobilising assent to them, even if they increase the powers of the European Parliament. No less important is to what extent European Union is a product of *social change* corresponding to the forces of nationalism that over the past two centuries inspired and sustained the movement for democracy in Europe, as well as in the great North American union. The question for us must be how does the process of forming new European political institutions differ from the earlier mostly very protracted, laborious and ultimately violent process of nation-building.

The recent interest in European integration as a process of social or cultural change was partly triggered by evidence of public scepticism, especially in response to the Maastricht treaty. Even professional administrators and jurists, who have as a class tended to supply the chief advocates of integration by the Community method, began to ask searching questions about the longer-term viability of a union built only on a slender constitutional framework provided by international treaty.

Probably the greatest shock for those directly involved in the practice and the teaching of European integration was caused in 1993 by the *Bundesverfassungsgericht* (the German federal constitutional court), which in an opinion on ratification of the Maastricht treaty cast doubt on the compatibility of further integration with the German constitution, and so brought the whole issue of the social prerequisites of legitimacy of supranational authorities into question. That opinion has led to much speculation among social scientists as well as lawyers as to whether genuinely democratic political institutions can develop on a European scale before a corresponding *demos*, or people sharing a common political identity, could also be said to have evolved. In other words, the German court and its juridical advisers might be interpreted as suggesting that the social conditions for the development of European Union into a genuine polity would be similar to those in which nation-states were formed in previous European experience.[28]

There has subsequently been much speculation about what kind of cultural changes might be necessary before there could be a genuine European government.[29] However, for reasons of both theory and practice (and included in the latter those of morality) speculations about a distinctive European identity, corresponding to the national identities that contributed so much to the construction of modern European nation-states, ought not to be countenanced. There are of course special historical reasons why every living European has the deepest possible moral obligation to resist any temptation to pursue such a train of thought, not to mention the prudential reasons in our own time why to try to build a political union of European peoples on the basis of ethnicity or culture could be only either suicidal or obscene. A pan-European identity palpably cannot be forged out of the social factors such as common language, religion or race, which proved so efficient and disastrous in the past.

In fact, and innocently enough, in contrast to the demonic forces of national integration in European experience, the concept of European identity has been used in the context of political union for the most part in terms of *external* relations, especially during the 1980s, in the procedures of European Political Cooperation, to describe a residual common position in foreign policy, which is assumed to remain when the differences between member states are excepted. The European Union has now also adopted many concerns, which it previously left to the Council of Europe, regarding common or shared culture in an even looser and innocuous sense, ranging from substantial projects of educational, youth and artistic exchanges to the paraphernalia of flag, anthem and insignia. None of these aspects, nor that of the 'common cultural heritage' imagined by the framers of the Maastricht treaty (Article 128), is, fortunately, relevant today to the questions of how much and what kind of social integration must be evident to support viable political institutions of government, and whether the requisite amount and kind have yet evolved in the European Union.

It is nevertheless vitally important to address the question of a European *demos* and get it right. What matters more than anything else in this respect is to recognise actual or potential social deprivation and injustice on a significant scale in Europe and to create adequate political means to fight for its redress.

How one might usefully compare with national integration is to ask why the European Union cannot inspire the same sense of personal security, material and psychological, that people in modern Europe have come to associate with the nation-state, especially in its reformed version as the welfare state that became the norm for most of Europe following the Second world war.[30] The crucial missing link of democracy in European Union is the absence of what recent commentators have variously described as the social cohesion, solidarity, loyalty or allegiance that have happened in our own time and region, when public power has been used benignly for the economic and social improvement of the masses.[31]

One place, if not *the* place to look for evidence of this kind of development on a European scale must be the European Parliament. Indeed, we might well be tempted to wonder whether, without evidence that such a social constituency has evolved, the European Parliament has any legitimate claim to the status of parliament at all. Hence the following:

THEOREM 6 *THE EUROPEAN PARLIAMENT PROVIDES A CHANNEL OF REPRESENTATION FOR VITAL SOCIAL FORCES THAT CANNOT ACHIEVE FULFILMENT THROUGH NATIONALISM AND THE NATION-STATE.*

If we can imagine the existence of real motivations, interests, even personal case histories, better still discernible groups, any of which does not require a presumption of the nation-state's monopoly of legitimate political authority and may indeed hold a deep suspicion or resentment of such a monopoly, and of all the multiple forms of economic and social organisation of which it is the ultimate origin — where better to look for it than an institution formally endowed with the unique function and competence of representing the peoples of the European Union directly?

However, Theorem 6 clearly begs a number of crucial questions, some of which might be answered by means of appropriate empirical research:

- Do social forces of the kind adumbrated exist and are they conscious of the possibility of political action in a framework territorially and sociologically grander than the nation-state?

- Should we not understand by this concept far more than just the more obvious manifestations of transnational activity of a mainly commercial or political intent, including business corporations and sectional interest groups, as well as transnational organisations of political parties?

- Can the European Parliament provide adequate representation for these social forces, in terms of both its formal powers and the manner of its composition? (This question in turn begs a number of others concerning the use of powers, the system and procedure of election, and the internal organisation of parliament.)

- Even if transnational social forces do exist in the manner supposed here, would they necessarily seek or find expression through constitutional means, and not be too radical even for an unusual body like the European Parliament?

- Indeed, is the European Parliament the only, or even the main, place to look for manifestations of such new sorts of political allegiance and action?

We should not expect these European *forces vives* to be merely reproductions of the parties and interest groups that have been designed in response to government exclusively by nation-states. Therefore, the political groups that play such a decisive role in the European Parliament now might not be adequate to represent such new social forces. Despite a series of direct elections, there is still not enough evidence yet to say whether these groups may be embryonic political parties, capable of acting within a distinct sphere of supranational politics. The fact that each of the groups, at least all the larger and more durable ones, usually contain representatives of all or most member states is not a sufficient reason to conclude that political organisation is adequately developed at a European level to represent the popular rather than the national interest.

Members do not depend on a European political group for election or re-election and continue to owe allegiance, perhaps in many cases primarily, to national parties, or at least to their own national delegation within the group to which they belong.

Nevertheless, throughout its life the Parliament's effective organisation and development has depended on the leadership of a core of activists from different groups (mostly socialist, Christian and liberal). These have often been elder statesmen with rich experience of European affairs in other venues, strongly committed to integration by the Community method, most of them declared federalists. This federalist coalition — almost a shadow party — has always been able to command support of a solid majority among the Parliament's total membership, especially for votes on crucial constitutional issues. But it is relatively conservative, always reticent whenever Parliament's action might threaten the European project as a whole. Although its leading personalities have changed over time, its leaders are not usually of a type to offer much inspiration as *forces vives*. Perhaps one reason why they appear so merely quixotic, is that their natural opposition, the anti-federalists (mainly national personalities from Britain, Denmark and France especially) have always managed to avoid a confrontation on the same ground.

If the Parliament fails to give the appearance of a vanguard of democratic social redress, it is on account less of aversion among its own membership than of indifference. However, absenteeism in an institution of this peculiar nature has many explanations, one of which may be the absorption of members with business both more particular and more practical than what goes in the plenary. European representatives who devote most of their energies to defending and promoting the interests of constituents, in both a territorial and a functional sense, might be, even unwittingly, constructing a new space of political action, beyond the state, though this might demand of them a degree of specialisation and of disengagement from group politics internal to the Parliament.

We need to know more, therefore, about the multiple relationships between members and their constituencies in this broader sense, which includes both pressure groups (promoting some cause for the public good) and interest groups (protecting a sectional and mainly economic investment). Those relationships might well be working, in accordance with the Madisonian principle, to counteract some species of 'majority tyranny' in the states. They might be promoting some benefit foregone, or exposing some cost otherwise hidden, as an effect of state sovereignty. Let us, by analogy with economic science call it: dealing with an *externality* of the use of public power by states.

However, the evidence of lobbies seeking and obtaining access to the European Parliament is not enough to prove that MEPs serve a unique and otherwise disenfranchised constituency of interests. Private organisations and individuals acting as intermediaries, sometimes employed directly by particular firms, on behalf of commercial or other sectional interests, have by definition other, usually more profitable, means of influencing the use of public power. Even highly-populated occupational or professional groups such as farmers, medical practitioners or accountants, with members on whom large numbers of others also depend for a livelihood, if only as family dependants, tend to be single-minded and pragmatic in their dealings with public authority. Such organisations of economic self-interest would indeed normally be happy, other things being equal, to rely on their existing connections with national governments and administrations, to which for the most part they owe their very origins. The point is, of course, that now, as a result of European integration by the Community method, other things have been made unequal by the prohibition of most uses of public power by states to protect and promote sectional economic interests.

To the extent that the organisations of manufacturers, traders, bankers and financiers, farmers and members of the liberal professions have constructed the same kind of symbiotic relationship with public authority at European level as they have done within most European states, it may be more on account of their continuing relationship with state administration than of any new links with supranational institutions, especially the European Parliament. We should examine whether these sectional interests have the potential to be numbered among the vital forces of a new European constituency: it is after all well known that they have been mobilised by the Commission to play a vital role in economic integration.[32]

The representation of local communities and regions within states is a rather different matter. More often than not this type of special interest, primarily differentiated territorially rather than functionally, represents within itself a kind of general interest, each subnational community being to some extent a microcosm, but one that will imply needs and opportunities liable to be neglected by the state and even to be marginalised by it (derelict inner cities as much as under-developed rural peripheries). Add to this the aspirations of culturally distinct communities, some of them eligible to be nations within nations, and we find a significant species of minority, plural within as well as among states throughout Europe, and clearly disadvantaged, even oppressed for some time previously, by the predominance of the nation-state.

The most substantial European constituency could materialise as nothing less than the vast majority of people living in the member states as workers, consumers, family dependants, involuntarily unemployed and unwaged, who have in theory a strong motive to be better represented at a supranational level in order to redress the previous balance in the use of public power in favour of sectional interests. For example, how much did the European Parliament contribute to the coalition of forces that supported the concerted promotion of the 'social dimension' during the 1980s? There is some evidence that such a loose, mostly informal coalition existed during that decade, and maybe subsequently, involving centrally the Commission's presidency, encompassing certain states' governments acting in Council and its ancillary bodies, the ETUC and other interest groups, and also engaging a more or less concerted action by the main political groups in Parliament, especially the socialists.

Another, even more suggestive possibility is that the European Parliament might be a vehicle for new movements or groups that have been marginalised, or otherwise under-represented by the nation-state, up to now. Anthony Giddens suggests that the conditions of late modernity in an advanced society like that of contemporary Europe give rise to a generic and historic shift in the agenda of politics from 'emancipatory politics' towards moral and existential issues of 'life politics'. At the same time there is a corresponding broadening and opening of political discourse from issues related mainly to the state, as the great modern issues of political, economic and cultural freedom famously were, to those arising from more general and fundamental conflicts of value, which are universalistic in nature and which the nation-state is inappropriate or simply geographically too confined to resolve.

Many of the issues of the social dimension of European integration in the broader sense may be seen as falling into this category, certainly those concerning the effects on the quality of life of environmental pollution and other external costs of economic activity self-regulated by markets, and even those dealing with conditions of employment, especially such issues as the enhancement of work opportunities through education, training and technological innovation and the right *not* to work (regulation of working hours, overtime, retirement, etc.).

Other potential issues of a similar type might be: local economic development and self-reliance; the limits of scientific and technological innovation, for example in genetic engineering; the private and public uses of violence; freedom in gender and sexual predisposition; the rights of migrants, both voluntary and involuntary, linking with discussion of new conceptions of citizenship; and the countervailing rights of privacy and publicity. It is not so much that there is evidence of a significant demand for such issues to be resolved by establishing uniform legislative standards, or that this would be appropriate at a European level of public authority, but rather that there is reason to suspect that the state-centred view of politics may distort and even deny them.[33] A major part of what is involved may be simply a latent demand for the civilised being's essential multiplicity of identity to be allowed to break out of the constraints of nationalism and escape the oppression imposed by sovereignty.

These speculations suggest, at least, that *social* integration may have a deeper and greater relevance than has so far been adequately recognised, even in the earlier campaign for developing a social dimension to the European Community. Habermas uses just this terminology to evoke those forces of solidarity, common identity and civic practice, arising from the *Lebenswelt*, or all that which may be seen as excluded by the modern functionalist view of political action as primarily instrumental or strategic to the maintenance of a system. The 'public sphere' (*Öffentlichkeit*) required for the expression and fulfilment of those forces clearly transcends the nation-state, though this may appear as the only political framework so far to have allowed integration at all successfully in modern conditions. Perhaps the European Parliament, seen from a broader sociological and historical perspective, may be the ideal venue for a truly integrative communicative discourse; and all the more because in the systematically comparative sense it is not a parliament. Nevertheless, there must be more to such a vision than sociological or philosophical speculation: the economic, legal and political must still have due priority to the extent that what is essentially at issue is the control, limitation and ultimately reclamation of the use of public power.

It seems reasonable to assume that the introduction of direct elections must have helped to increase concern for the more numerous groups that are exceptionally dependant on public power: those of us in the vast majority of any nation or none who need access to the labour market for subsistence, those — in effect the same people — involuntarily exposed to the harmful effects of industrial and agricultural pollution and the risks of faulty manufacture and processing, mendacious and fraudulent commercial and professional practice, as well as those of us who cannot afford our own protection against the effects of old age, sickness, disaster and death.

Nevertheless, if these majority interests were so important as we must assume them to be, then why did the European Parliament not go to even greater lengths on their behalf? If the interests concerned could be sufficiently protected by the nation-state, and those engaged in electoral politics at a European level thought so too, then we might well ask why the fuss about European democracy in the first place. If the European Parliament is not the main channel of representation for those social forces whose essential needs and interests transcend the national boundary, then why not?

6. The Use Of Public Power

Is there a specific constituency of the European Union? If there were, it would be recognisable not only in the European representation of opinions and interests that tend to be distorted, neglected or even suppressed by national representation, but also in a distinctively European *configuration of power*. The various attitudes, opinions, motivations and aspirations that would make up such a constituency would not just take form spontaneously. They would not indeed be revealed formally or even potentially in the evidence of statistical social surveys or opinion polls.[34] They would take on political meaning only after they had developed a certain degree of organisation with the incentive and opportunity to influence the use of power in the public sphere.

Consequently, in order to judge what contribution the European Parliament makes to democracy, it is necessary to know what is its power, how it uses that power, and to what effect. If the European Parliament does not use power on behalf of a unique constituency, maybe that is because it is not capable of making use of public power in ways that are relevant to the aspirations and needs of those concerned. Therefore, when looking for evidence of a distinctively European constituency, *demos*, or civil society, we should examine how the European Parliament uses its own formal powers or 'competences', and also how it mobilises influence by means of persuasion, negotiation and exposure.

According to a hard rather than a soft definition of democracy, the public must be able to enjoy autonomy in effect and not only in terms of constitutional recognition and electoral self-expression. David Held's 'principle of autonomy' offers such a definition:

> 'persons should enjoy equal rights and, accordingly, equal obligations in the specification of the political framework which generates and limits the opportunities available to them; that is, they should be free and equal in the determination of the conditions of their own lives, so long as they do not deploy this framework to negate the rights of others.'[35]

Held applies this principle to the practice of democracy by suggesting various criteria for assessing people's ability to develop their personal capacities in relation to various 'sites of power'. Personal autonomy needs to be cultivated, and conversely defended, in multiple respects, not only in relation to the classical liberal, emancipatory issues such as freedom from physical constraint and abuse, of thought and expression, and of association. True democracy must provide additionally for positive rights and freedoms, which need the protection and enforcement of public power, including access to education, health and other collective provisions of welfare, and means of communication and cultural participation, as well as freedom from economic restraint and deprivation, from violence and coercion employed by the state (one's own state or others). In short, the individual's capacity to enjoy democracy depends to a significant extent on the defence and promotion of his or her basic needs of autonomy by the collective use of public power.[36]

However, there is a rather basic reason why we should not expect the European Parliament to be a venue of serious political contest over the sites of power, except in a relatively limited sense.

THEOREM 7 *THE EUROPEAN PARLIAMENT'S CAPACITY TO INFLUENCE AND CONTROL THE USE OF PUBLIC POWER IS LIMITED BY THE EUROPEAN UNION'S OWN CAPACITY TO DO THE SAME.*

In other words, as members and officials of the Parliament know from experience, their endeavours to redress grievances and promote well-being are often frustrated by the Union's lack of authority to act in the spheres concerned, or, even more frustrating, because the Union has been given responsibility but not power.

Most parliamentary institutions or legislatures are similarly restricted. The cause may be written or unwritten constitutional limitations on their own formal powers and all European states do impose such limitations. However, a common constraint is the insufficient capacity of the state itself to take effective action, on account of a lack of resources, the absence of compliance domestically or externally. To a large extent, the problem facing those who would want to make the European Parliament more efficient, in terms of a capacity to use power for the common good, is the same as that facing all political representatives at both national and European levels.

Not only have legislatures as a genre lost the position imagined for them in the classical versions of liberalism (at least partly because they have almost inevitably in conditions of modern democracy become agencies of the regime rather than of genuine opposition to the regime), but the liberal constitutional state itself has had to forfeit its historic role as 'the great legislator of mankind' and even as the unsurpassable protector and arbiter of the common good in the midst of human error and conflict. An increasingly topical way of interpreting this demise, or crisis of legitimacy, is to see it as justifying a growth or revival of interest in 'civil society', a term mostly used to refer vaguely and promiscuously to all social relations that do not include the state. I shall use it here more precisely to denote that autonomous sphere of social action that lies between the familial, on the hand, and the political, on the other (*bürgerliche Gesellschaft*).

One consequence of bringing civil society in this sense into the picture is that political struggle at the level of the European Union may be seen as both especially restricted and especially enabled on account of its distance from state power. Any investigation of the European Parliament's capacity to reduce systematically inequalities in the distribution of wealth and power, especially when these are structural, has, therefore, to allow for the ambivalence of Parliament's position in reality. In one more conventional sense (relating to the Union's lack of sovereignty), we should expect that distance to incapacitate Parliament, along with the Union as a whole. In another sense, however, the distance from state politics also situates Parliament potentially at the critical intersection of those forces of civil society that transcend the national sphere, not just because they evade the state's territorial borders but because they have an energy and a purpose of their own that defies the temporal intervention of the state.

Legislative power

Although the competence of the EU institutions is less truly legislative in the strict constitutional sense than regulatory, the EC treaty is a source of substantial regulatory competence that amounts in effect to a potentially far-reaching use of legislative power. Indeed, as Majone has demonstrated, the common market seems to have intensified a trend, already developing within states, to use public power for economic ends by means of indirect regulatory mechanisms rather than by direct participation or provision.[37] The substantial transfer of regulatory activity from the national to the European level may be seen as part of a general trend by states to transform the classical legislative power into a means of expanding the scope and the effects of public authority, enlarging its discretion, and reducing its real accountability. One consequence has been a very significant enlargement of the responsibility, but not necessarily the ability or the volition, to use legislative power to redress the balance between private and public interests, minority and majority. The danger is that European integration simply provides governments, and the economic interests attached to them, with a convenient alibi to pursue ends of their own choosing that might not be acceptable or feasible in purely domestic circumstances.[38]

Although the European Parliament has obtained significant power to determine how the Union manages its functions to regulate economic and social affairs, it really has very little means of determining what those functions should be. In that sense the legislative power at European level still belongs to the member states themselves, subject to whatever pressures happen to be most influential on them at any given time. How states use that power, and whether or not they use it, can make a substantial difference to the results of European integration in terms of the distribution of wealth between the groups and classes whose interests inevitably diverge in an advanced, post-industrial society.

From the experience of both the Maastricht and Amsterdam Treaties, member state governments would hardly seem the most responsible agencies for ensuring that the functions of public policy are allocated in the most rational, transparent and efficient manner. The way the member state governments have substantially added to the functions they themselves seek to exercise collectively outside the constitutional framework of the treaties itself provides further evidence of the alibi principle at work. A responsible use of legislative power at a European level would be not to enlarge the functions of the Union without ensuring that the functions transferred are subject to appropriate supervision and control, above all by those directly representing the interest of a majority of the people living in the member states.

Within the prevailing constitutional and political constraints, however, the European Parliament does at least have the power to ensure both that the regulatory decisions within its purview are efficiently and judiciously exercised in the public interest, and that the state governments are made accountable for their motives and actions when they seek to use legislative power beyond the national framework of public accountability.

Budgetary power

The European Parliament's use of that other great classical source of parliamentary influence and control, budgetary power also reflects the Union's own shortcomings. In terms of both size and content, there is relatively little power to get and spend money by means of the budget of the European Community. One major constraint is the lack of power either to raise additional revenue from existing sources or to introduce new sources of revenue without the unanimous agreement of the member states.

The most striking peculiarity of the European Union's budget, compared to that of any modern state, including federations, is that it is almost completely lacking in macroeconomic significance. This is not only because it is of relatively miniscule size (1.20% of total GNP of the 15-state Union in 1999), which is negligible in terms of any counter-cyclical effects it might have on aggregate employment, prices or incomes in the Union as a whole, but because of the highly restricted means available to the Union itself to finance expenditure at any level. In effect, like the legislative power, the fiscal power belongs to the member states, and again they are largely unaccountable for its exercise — or, no less importantly, for their failure to exercise it.

Moreover, not only does the Union lack fiscal power of its own, it has also eschewed so far anything more than a very indirect responsibility for fiscal policy. This too is still primarily within the ambit of the states themselves, though subject to two major limitations consequent on the decision to introduce monetary union. These are: first, the member states are now obliged to make their own overall budgetary decisions a matter of general concern, submitting them to a regular procedure of surveillance involving both the Commission and other states' governments in the Council, and conforming to a general prohibition on excessive deficits; and secondly, that participants in the common currency regime, which centralises the authority to determine the rates of exchange and interest, anyway lose a large measure of the flexibility they might otherwise have had (or claimed to have) to manage their national economies in accordance with a desired level of public expenditure.

EMU, like the transfer of regulatory powers, is best understood as continuing a trend towards the de-politicisation of economic affairs already begun within the states. To some extent, indeed, those who seek to govern in any advanced, industrialised country (except possibly the USA) are nowadays obliged by circumstances to admit a certain impotence in trying to manipulate economic activity in accordance with a national policy for economic development. Most specialists now seem to agree that, with or without participation in a common currency, European national governments have little to gain for any macroeconomic purpose from the use of fiscal power; they are too constrained both by the unpredictability of international trade and movements of capital and by domestic structural rigidities, especially in the labour market. Parliamentary control of economic policy seems more and more to be a chimera at any level.

The European Parliament has no direct part in the procedure of multilateral surveillance or in decisions to intervene when member states get into economic and therefore social difficulties. However, its views must be visibly taken into account when the rules governing these and certain other crucial procedures are made. Parliament also has a right to be informed about the decisions taken on economic policy at Union level, and has important functions to help safeguard the independence of the European Central Bank. Again, it has a vital, if constrained, task of ensuring maximum transparency, rectitude and clear allocation of responsibility. It is likely that MEPs will have to be inventive and determined in the use of what powers they have if EMU is to be a popular success.[39]

The European budget also lacks another dimension that was historically very much associated with the evolution of democracy, and one in which national parliaments once played a major role. There seems to be little serious possibility of using fiscal power at European level to pursue a policy of re-distribution of income. Proposals to establish autonomous programmes of inter-personal financial transfers, as opposed to transfers of financial resources between states for specified objectives of public policy by means of the 'structural funds', have always been resisted and, perhaps surprisingly, never seriously championed by any major grouping in the European Parliament. One explanation is that, since the 1980s, re-distributive and counter-cyclical fiscal policies, along with direct income supports such as unemployment benefit, have lost popularity compared to programmes for creating and facilitating employment.

Parliament's budgetary powers partly account for decisions to increase the amount and vary the type of expenditures allocated from the budget to the structural funds for regional and social policies, as well as leading to the inclusion of several minor, additional funds for overseas aid and humanitarian causes, though they must also take some responsibility for the perpetuation of relatively high levels of spending on the CAP. Nevertheless, such decisions to re-allocate (or not) available revenue by means of the budget is much less important that the ability to question, say, the balance of expenditure throughout the Union between, for example, surplus grain production and the stockpile of armaments. Of course, the Parliament does not do this because the Union has no say over defence policy. But such an issue may rationally be considered relevant to the economic efficiency and equity with which public power is deployed in the Union as a whole. Again, the issue of Parliament's power cannot be separated from that of the Union itself; and the reluctance of states to be accountable for their own expenditures is a greater obstacle to the Union's overall capacity to attain an equitable and efficient allocation of resources than its mere lack of revenue.

Common foreign and security policy

If there is one respect more than any other in which the European Parliament is disabled from influencing or controlling the use of public power for the common good, it is with respect to foreign policy and the inevitably related issues of national security (both external and internal). State parliaments are themselves of course also most constrained in these same respects. The causes are fundamental and to some extent insuperable.

The assertion of national interest without or within the boundaries of the state, is a classic function of executive power, as well as its primary justification. Of course, a genuine threat to either external or internal security can by its very nature be adequately confronted only by commission (even if, as has occurred in famous historical cases, parliament itself identifies the threat and instigates the response, maybe against the sovereign power itself). The kind of commission — soldier or diplomat, clerk or executioner — should fit the circumstances of the case. Of course, it is the mark of good administration, if in the normal course of events, or at least so long as fortune is not offended, such emergencies are avoided; but a community is unlikely to be blessed with this happy condition unless it is also blessed with a virtuous prince or a parliament capable of finding and sustaining one.

With its new power to approve the appointment of the Commission, Parliament may even now be considered capable of choosing a virtuous prince. The problem is of course is that in most crucial respects the prince is almost naked and the violator's hands already approach what flimsy underwear remains. Member states have insisted in effect that, despite their having entered into a quasi-federal relationship with each other in some respects, they each still retain enough separate political identity, not to say sovereignty, to assert their own national interests by means of foreign policy. All the more paradoxical is it, therefore, that they should have sought to make this assertion most forcibly and visibly by claiming to have established a *common* foreign and security policy (CFSP) among themselves. So far, however, this consists mainly of a set of objectives and procedures, and lacks substantive powers or an agency capable of deploying them, including the expenditure of human and material resources. Indeed, the real purpose of the CFSP is to enable the member states to ensure that nothing can be effectively done by the Union in the sphere of foreign policy and security without their own unanimous prior consent.[40]

The European Parliament is severely restricted in relation to CFSP, not only because its formal powers are limited to those of being informed and making non-binding recommendations, but more especially since it has no means of doing anything positive that the member states are not already willing to do beyond the adoption of well-meaning resolutions, sending goodwill delegations of its own members on missions abroad, and the insertion of new headings in the budget to pay for humanitarian assistance.

Procedurally, the Commission, the only agency that could act effectively on Parliament's behalf, now has the formal power to submit proposals to Council on any questions relating to the CFSP, and there is nothing to prevent it formulating them out of Parliament's own resolutions. However, no such proposal is likely to get anywhere unless it conforms to the principles and guidelines already forged by the heads of member state governments in the European Council, while the Commission would be bound to need the active support of at least a large majority of member states, if only to obtain the means necessary to implement the proposal.[41]

State parliaments may feel themselves no less impotent, especially when the governments accountable to them do not have at their disposal any significant economic and military means of influencing or repelling the actions of foreign powers. If so, then the CFSP can hardly be said to have improved their position and may have weakened it. It has not reduced the dependence of states that lack economic or military resources on those that have them, while the latter are as yet under no obligation to use those resources as a consequence of CFSP (although they are under just such an obligation through their prior commitment to Nato).

Nevertheless, the European Parliament is endowed with formal powers that do correspond to those conventionally used by national parliaments to control the management of national security, in so far as they find it practical or desirable to do so at all. Some of these it obtained only recently, like the right to prevent the coming into force without its assent of treaties or other international agreements between the Union and non-members or the accession of non-members. Others originated with the founding treaties or acts almost as long-standing, such as the right to question both Commission and Council on the exercise of their various executive powers and the right to censure the former with the sanction of dismissal, or the limited power to approve the Community budget, without which neither domestic nor foreign adventure can be afforded. Indeed, in so far as the other common institutions have always had some responsibility for external relations, the European Parliament in its turn had or has eventually acquired the limited means typically available to parliaments to supervise and encourage their good management (and, since the treaty enjoins free movement of trade, capital and labour between states, this might be said to apply to responsibility for internal relations bearing on security as well).

Parliament's disability in relation to external and internal security above all, but also with respect to other vital aspects of good government, is that public policy within the Union still largely evades the constitutional limitations written into the Community treaties, on which the Parliament's own power essentially depends. While member states claim the freedom to enter into alternative and additional international agreements by treaty or otherwise, among themselves or with others, and assert the right to pursue cooperation or integration while eschewing federalism and excluding themselves or others from any agreements that result from such a process, the Union cannot be regarded as establishing a constitutional or federal order, and hence must continue to lack an adequate provision for democracy, parliamentary or otherwise.

Although this discussion of CFSP raises some highly controversial issues that cannot be pursued adequately here, it serves to underline an important general observation, which applies to public policy in general. This is that the inclusion of new spheres of public policy by means of new treaties and expanding thereby the Union's functions, does not necessarily increase parliamentary influence and control, at European or national levels, and may actually reduce them, at either or both of those levels. In other words, the converse of Theorem 7 is not true. There is, nonetheless, an obverse that is true, though many have ignored it to their loss and that of the causes they represent: that whenever and however the European Union's capacity to use public power is expanded, the European Parliament is a necessary (though not necessarily sufficient) means of preventing its abuse.

7. Conclusions: From Model To Real

This report is intended as the first of a series of research papers which will investigate different aspects of representative democracy within the European Union. I have tried here to clarify the key concepts and simplify, as far as possible, the results of previous research and theorising, though with a largely non-academic, but informed and educated, readership in view and without treating any of the main issues or arguments in the depth that would be due to them in a normal academic paper. It may be useful here to give a very brief summary of the seven theorems that I have deployed in an effort to remove the obscuration and delusion that usually cloud perceptions of the real conditions in which the European Parliament has to perform and also in a preliminary way to present a clearer vision of the objectives and principles to which that institution might realistically aspire. It will be up to later studies to deal with any remaining obscurities and to say how realistic that vision might be.

I began, for reasons pertaining to issues much larger than European integration, by asserting that it was pointless to study the European Parliament as if it were a normal political institution, classifiable in comparative politics, or as if the European Union were a political system. Indeed, it is our very compulsion to want to classify and define the Parliament in this way that causes its role to be so irritatingly ambivalent and vague **(Theorem 1)**. As I concluded from a similar study published twenty years ago, the European Parliament should not look to the parliaments in European nation-states for a model, chiefly because both in the model-building of political scientists and the behaviour of practitioners, 'parliamentary democracy is more comprehensible as a set of ideas than as a record of practice ...'.[42] To restrict the future possibilities to a mere copy of what is done now would be to disregard other vital characteristics and issues that give this so-called parliament quite enough opportunity to contribute to the peace and contentment of people everywhere without even addressing the issue whether it does or might belong to a political system and of what kind.

The second main point follows from the danger that treating the EU as if it were or could be a state and the European Parliament as if it were a parliament, which it is not and ought not want to be, obscures and even obstructs the genuine responsibility of actual states and their actual parliaments. It is the responsibility first and foremost of national states and parliaments to provide for democracy, and it is they who should be blamed for any deficit of democracy in European or national politics **(Theorem 2)**. If there are genuine problems of democracy in the performance of European Union then the first place to look for both cause and remedy should be the member states themselves. Even a truly federal European Union could only be as democratic as the states constituting it **(Theorem 3)**. To the extent that 'political integration' has, in fact, proceeded at the expense of integration in a true sense, of social cohesion and solidarity and other qualities necessary to the building of community, then the moral is literally that charity begins at home: future investigation into the cause of the 'democratic deficit' might well concentrate on the common tendency of states to make the Union an alibi for their own shortcomings and misdemeanours.

This observation connects nicely with the classical theory of federalism, which in turn has an extremely relevant contemporary application, usually ignored or pre-judged as irrelevant, to remedy the inevitable shortcomings of international relations from the perspective of democracy and its prior condition, constitutionalism. The Madisonian principles — that federal government is both a requisite subsidiary to democracy in states **(Theorem 4)** and a necessary condition of it **(Theorem 5)** — expounded in *The Federalist* over 200 years ago, apply forcibly to the EU's current needs, in view both of its recently expanded competence and of its anticipated further enlargement to include states with special historical reasons to welcome the guarantee of democracy provided by genuinely parliamentary institutions at a supranational level. However, these are not the only grounds for constitutionalism in the EU, nor are the peoples of central and eastern Europe the only likely beneficiaries of it. The interesting question is why historically the sovereignty of nation-states proved as defensible as it did, so that only a very limited direct relationship between the European institutions and the people has been able to develop so far.

This leads to the next link in my argument which denies the increasingly fashionable but facile and false assumption that the impossibility at least in foreseeable conditions of a veritable European nationalism prevents genuine democracy and suggests instead that the problem of democracy may itself be an alibi for the preemptive and much more fundamental resistance of economic and political forces to the project of *social integration* initiated previously by the European Community, but doubtless doomed to failure. It is suggested that future research take as a starting point the hypothesis that a distinctively European constituency for the European Parliament does exist, but has not so far been adequately mobilised on account of the neglect of social integration **(Theorem 6)**. Perhaps the next paper planned for this series, in which Michael Steed will focus on choice and representation in the EU, might throw more light on the validity of this proposition and what guides to action might be derived from it.

Finally, the present paper offers a partial answer to this very question by pointing out the limitations of the use of public power by the European Union as itself a basic constraint on the European Parliament's effectiveness in mobilising a European constituency by responding to the real social needs of a majority of people living in the member states **(Theorem 7)**. This brings us back to the constitutional issue, in so far as only further constitutional reform can provide the Union or its Parliament with the necessary powers to become effective instruments of social change. Further papers in this series will also examine the shortcomings of existing powers and how these might be exercised more effectively, including Parliament's new power of co-decision, its role as a litigant before the Court of Justice, and the issue of forming an agenda for the next intergovernmental conference on treaty revision.

Self-styled federalists in the early postwar years campaigned for a constituent assembly, to be elected by the peoples of Europe and empowered by their governments to formulate a constitutional settlement and submit it for popular approval. Altiero Spinelli's initiative to persuade the first directly-elected European Parliament to prepare, and then in February 1984 adopt, a Draft Treaty on European Union was in its own way a revival of that earlier, abortive project. Parliament has continued to assume a constituent function, and we have seen that without doing so in some form it is admitting to virtual powerlessness in the face of the legislative power states have effectively requisitioned by their own collective action at a European level, now formalised as European Union.

However, there is not a great deal the European Parliament can do to defend the principles of constitutionalism. Unlike a classical parliament it has formal power neither to make constitutional or legislative proposals (in so far as the treaties can be amended only on the proposal of member states or the Commission), nor to prevent their adoption as amendments to the existing treaties (a right that belongs exclusively to the member states), while there is also nothing Parliament can do to prevent the established constitutional framework being undermined by other actions of all or some member states. It has, nevertheless, skilfully used what influence it has, chiefly through its right to be consulted, and by the moral pressure of being a directly-elected representative assembly, to help protect the existing institutional framework and enhance its own formal powers where this is appropriate.

Indeed, the way Parliament has performed this constituent function indicates how it can be more effective in building social cohesion without pretending to the impracticable and probably unnecessary role of constituent assembly. For one thing, there is much that could be beneficially achieved by means of the European constitution as it is while avoiding the needless risk of further intergovernmental conferences.

The future studies would be of great practical value if they could identify steps that the Parliament could take after the 1999 elections, building on what it has done up to now, though perhaps more because it proved to be the only expedient course rather than part of a pre-determined strategy. The general, operational principle should continue to be to strive for the greatest possible and most efficient *coalition of interests* across both state boundaries and political divisions, as well as between the EU institutions themselves. This is the method by which the Parliament is able to exercise a power well in excess of what is possible by its own means. Three possible aspects of this coalition strategy need to be clarified.

1. Coalition between political formations within the European Parliament

The main question is how, while allowing a solid, central majority to emerge on most crucial issues to do with the constitutional and political development of the Union, including especially the Parliament's own powers, there can still be room for divisions that reflect major cleavages in European society itself. Divisions within the Parliament on ideological or class lines, for example, should sometimes be matched with similar divisions between ministers of corresponding political persuasions in Council. They then have the advantage of emphasising the European, rather than purely national, dimension of the issue concerned. Coalitions should then be formed across the institutions rather than within them. There is a risk otherwise that both intra-institutional and inter-institutional consensus will provide alibis for those who desert the struggle for social redress.

2. *Subsidiarity and the role of national parliaments*

It should not be assumed that even the onset of a single market and single money need or should deprive states of the capacity to use legislative and fiscal power for many important economic and social ends.[43] It is clearly not to be expected or desired that states should give up the bulk of their existing responsibility for public administration (unless they give it up to subnational regional and local authorities). National parliaments will continue to be prime movers in these respects. Moreover, where states continue to maintain alliances, including military alliances, with non-member states and find it possible and convenient to allow their citizens to enjoy also special economic relationships overseas, especially in the form of foreign direct investment, then only national parliaments are in a position to hold them accountable, including the task of reminding governments of alternative policies.

The European Parliament can thus practise coalition with national parliaments, using its existing powers to check and make transparent the actions of governments at Union level. Some national parliaments, especially those in the smaller or economically weaker or more neutralist states may well find the European Parliament a valuable alternative to action by means of intergovernmental diplomacy, in which they are more likely, if not to be outnumbered, then certainly to be outmanoeuvred and outgunned. To exploit this kind of coalition-building could ease the problems of numerical representation of states in Parliament and Commission, and of weighting of votes in Council.

However, it makes no sense to give national parliaments additional representation at European level alongside the Council. It is astonishing that such a step can have been seriously proposed without first making a systematic comparison of the experience of the European Parliament itself before and after direct elections, in order to ascertain precisely what difference might be made by having a nominated in addition to an elected parliament.[44] The result would most likely show not a lot, except for the personal benefit to travelling members and the expedience for national party managers of disposing of some MPs temporarily while rewarding others.

3. *The politics of executive power*

No parliamentary body, including the US Congress, can be at all effective in terms of government without the concurrence of executive agency. However, the latter does not always have to work directly in response to parliament's will, and may be more efficacious in the interests of democracy should it enjoy a certain independence. Although there may be a tendency in the European Union towards a plurality of executive agencies, and although this may have some advantages over a single executive, the efficient use of executive power has its own constraints. The European Parliament can do much to enhance its own effectiveness, and compensate for its own shortcomings, by using its own power in coalition with that of the Commission.

It is, indeed, vitally important for the Parliament and for European democracy that the Commission should retain and develop its own position as the overarching, permanent executive authority at the level of the Union. To the extent that Parliament and Commission work together, even in collusion, the power of each to act for the common good is greatly enlarged, while to the extent that they neglect to do so, it is dissipated. There is no alternative method or agency of promoting positive actions for economic and social improvement, or for genuinely protecting security, when these need to be taken on behalf of the people of the Union as a whole. Experiments with other types of commission, especially of more transient or personalised or disestablished nature, and especially when composed of ministers or officials of state governments or their plenipotentiaries, cannot perform the same function, and can serve only as substitutes for positive action, disguising one or more of duplicity, pusillanimity, procrastination and incompetence. Bad government is usually made of these, whether the matter in hand be the coordination of fiscal policy or the management of external relations. Persistent attempts to find an alternative to the Commission, or in whatever way to dilute its capacity, or frustrate the development of a genuine European civil service, are seriously misguided.

One method by which the Parliament can act pragmatically to enhance its own and the overall capacity is to make tactical use of its own newly enlarged right to approve the appointment of the Commission President (who then must in turn approve the appointment of the other members, according to Article 214 of the Treaty of Amsterdam) in order to ensure that only a personality endorsed by a majority of the European electorate can be chosen to lead the Union's only permanent and ubiquitous executive. Such a tactic is available if one or more coalitions of parties, represented in the Parliament, will take this step for another, or others to follow. Member state governments would then be hard put not to select the candidate already endorsed by a subsequent elected majority of the Parliament. And the new President thus appointed would carry an authority that none of his or her predecessors have been able to claim.

It is vitally important that by methods such as these the European Parliament can build on its past achievements, mixed as these have been with disappointment and distraction, to demonstrate that the political importance of EMU lies neither in its paving the way for the realisation of some new ideal construction or would-be polity, nor merely in its contribution to facilitating the commercial performance of producers and investors. Such a project must concentrate primarily, therefore, on ensuring that the re-distributive, reproductive and more broadly ecological consequences of economic activity are suitably managed for the sake of social cohesion.

This was a focus that was far easier to maintain when the original European Communities were founded nearly half a century ago. Such a project was then far more manageable not only thanks to the small number of states willing or able to belong but also because those states, acting individually or collectively, were no longer in a position realistically to assume in full the conventional ambitions of a nation-state, especially with regard to external relations and security. The role of European states, with regard to such matters and to classical statecraft in any form, was deeply constrained by the conditions of Cold War, and in the west were in most cases superseded by support for or abstention from the North Atlantic Alliance. The gradually increasing temptation to be more pretentious and more iconographic, as the Community enlarged its membership, turned into an irresistible compulsion in the 1990s, when the end of the Cold War removed a major cause of both old divisions, including those of German sovereignty, and more recent extra-European alliances.

It is, therefore, a tragic irony that the otherwise gracious liberation of what had become Europe's most cruel and intractable border, that between west and east, should have become for those who work for the integration of Europe a problem mainly of security. However, the new exposure of both western and eastern Europe to new prospects of self-reliance and new possibilities of self-aggrandisement, has now challenged directly the ambivalence of integration. It is no longer possible to evade the issue whether the project of European Union is or is not a classic scheme of the politics of power, primarily occupied with the construction or defence of boundaries, whether of domains or of identities, of states or of nations, of classes or of ideas. There can no longer be any doubt about the sheer error of that alleged theory of political change which sought to justify economic functionalism only as an accelerator of political unification. What has imposed on us all the spectre of political union in the classical sense is not economic or even monetary integration but the implosion of those forces of terror which managed to hold the world, and especially Europe, in thrall for forty years after the second world war.

Whether it is resolved by means of enlargement of European Union towards the east, or by some other more or less lasting expedient, the crisis consequential on the end of the strategic postwar division and pacification of Europe matters more than anything else for the future welfare and security of the peoples of the European Union. The greatest danger for them is that the crisis becomes an opportunity to revive in full the previously customary European practice of politics as war by other means, especially in the politics between nations. Accession to the Union of even some of the states in central and eastern Europe now seeking it will cause problems of adaptation greater than ever before, because of both the quantitative and qualitative effects. It could prove to be the end altogether of the civilising, liberalising, communitarian, innovative, pragmatic mission courageously and inspiringly begun by the resistance to fascism over fifty years ago.

If by the time the first set of accessions comes about the anarchy of intergovernmentalism will have infiltrated more deeply into the processes by which the Union tries to govern itself, then the enlargement of membership can only exacerbate its deleterious effects. Intergovernmentalism would add greatly to the complexity and inflexibility of all procedures of decision and administration, and bring even closer that moment when it will be necessary to resort to a hegemonic order — in which a few larger states rule the multiple remainder — secured moreover only under threat of an ultimate but legitimate use of violence, which itself will probably not be wholly or even mainly European.

On the other hand, the problem that the liberation of central and eastern Europe poses to the Union cannot be resolved by either re-drawing boundaries or improving their defence. The problem is partly that two distinct spheres of contrasting economic performance cannot co-exist peacefully side-by-side in Europe, however efficiently the boundary between them is policed. It is also that the borders of Europe will nevertheless always be artificial and consequently always disputable, so long as they are economic and social rather than purely territorial and administrative. This is why it is now absolutely vital for the European Parliament to act as an integral but interdependent part of a constitutional and federal government, which provides the only available hope that the inevitable dissolution (or undermining) of the borders will happen peacefully and without destroying the precious autonomy that, after a millennium of struggle within and without, the diverse peoples of Europe may at last be in sight of claiming for themselves.

Postface

THEOREM 1

The European Parliament's role is ambivalent and indefinable to the extent that it does not belong to a typical national or international system.

THEOREM 2

The powers of national parliaments in relation to the European Union is a function primarily of the constitutional and political conditions prevailing within each state.

THEOREM 3

The practice of democracy by the member states is a necessary condition of its practice by the European Union.

THEOREM 4

The practice of democracy in each member state is not a sufficient condition of its practice in the European Union.

THEOREM 5

The practice of democracy at the level of the European Union is a necessary condition of its practice within the member states.

THEOREM 6

The European Parliament provides a channel of representation for vital social forces that cannot achieve fulfilment through nationalism and the nation-state.

THEOREM 7

The European Parliament's capacity to influence and control the use of public power is limited by the European Union's own capacity to do the same.

Notes

Chapter 1

[1] Michel Foucault, *This Is Not a Pipe,* trans. J. Harkness, Berkeley: University of California Press, 1982, p. 54.

[2] Jean-François Lyotard uses this fable as a way of illustrating the impossibility of satisfactorily defining the boundaries or the content of any system, *La Condition Postmoderne*, Paris: Les Editions de Minuit, 1979, pp. 90-91.

[3] Jean Baudrillard, *Simulacra and Simulations*, trans. Paul Foss et. al., New York: Semiotexte, 1983, pp. 1-13.

[4] See Andrew Duff (ed.), *The Treaty of Amsterdam: text and commentary*, London: Federal Trust with Sweet and Maxwell, 1997.

Chapter 2

[5] Richard Corbett, Francis Jacobs and Michael Shackleton, *The European Parliament*, third edition, London: Cartermill, 1995, p. 2.

[6] Zygmund Bauman, *Modernity and Ambivalence*, Cambridge: Polity Press, 1991, p. 1.

[7] See Leon N. Lindberg and Stuart A. Scheingold, *Europe's Would-be Polity: patterns of change in the European Community*, Englewood Cliffs, NJ: Prentice-Hall, 1970. This usage betrayed a failure to understand the place of integration in the very theorising about social systems from which it was supposedly derived. In Parson's seminal classification of social systems, the 'function' of the political sub-system was 'goal attainment', whereas 'integration' was the function assigned to the sub-system of 'normative control'. 'Integration theorists', however, have always talked about 'economic integration' and 'political integration' not only as if social integration could be achieved by economic or political action alone, but also as if these were apparently autonomous, though ultimately linked by the process of 'spillover'. See Talcott Parsons, *The Social System*, Glencoe, Ill.: Free Press, 1967; Lindberg and Scheingold (eds), *Regional Integration: theory and research*, Cambridge, Mass.: Harvard University Press, 1971. For different critiques of systems theory, including the German version developed mainly by Luhman, see Lyotard op. cit. and Jurgen Habermas, *Theorie des kommunikativen Handelns,* 2 vols, Frankfurt: Suhrkamp, 1981, trans. Thomas McCarthy as *The Theory of Communicative Action*, 2 vols, Cambridge: Polity Press, 1987; and *Der Philosophische Diskurs der Moderne*, Frankfurt: Suhrkamp, 1985, trans. Frederick G. Lawrence as *The Philosophical Discourse of Modernity*, Cambridge: Polity Press,1987.

[8] Hence the harmful deception implied, even if not intended, by the title of Neill Nugent's textbook, *The Government and Politics of the European Community*, 3rd edition, Basingstoke: Macmillan, 1994.

[9] Michael L. Mezey, 'Parliament in the new Europe', in Jack Hayward and Edward C. Page (eds), *Governing the New Europe*, Cambridge: Polity Press, 1995, p. 198. In his treatment of parliament, or 'the legislature', as a 'dependent variable' in the comparative government of European states, Mezey relates all the changes in its status and powers that he finds in recent European experience to wider systemic transformations (pp. 198-200).

[10] Philip Norton (ed.), *Parliaments in Western Europe*, London: Frank Cass, 1990, pp. 143-51.

[11] For the best analysis of these and other different perspectives, see Helen Wallace and William Wallace (eds), *Policy Making in the European Community*, 3rd edition, Chichester: John Wiley, 1996, pp. 439-60.

[12] The ambiguity was doubtless intended, a possibility ignored by Simon Bulmer and Wolfgang Wessels (*The European Council: decision-making in European politics*, Basingstoke: Macmillan, 1987) who also describe this body as an institution (which it is neither in a strictly legal nor a loosely sociological sense) - another unfortunate use of analogy by political scientists, by which so many students, now civil servants or even ministers, have been deceived.

[13] A. Moravcsik, 'Negotiating the Single European Act' in *International Organisation,* vol. 45, no. 1, 1991, pp.19-56; and 'Preferences and Power in the European Community: a liberal intergovernmentalist approach' in *Journal of Common Market Studies*, vol. 31, no. 4, 1992, pp. 473-524.

Chapter 3

[14] The first direct elections by universal suffrage took place in June 1979, although not according to a uniform electoral procedure, as the Treaty anticipated under the terms of Article 138.3.

[15] Those provisions (Articles 138.1 and 2 of the EEC Treaty) lapsed when elections were introduced in 1979.

[16] The Dutch, however, were particularly exercised about parliamentary power when the EEC treaty was being negotiated and raised the same issue again - though their concern was then mixed with pecuniary considerations - during their 1965 row with the French over the methods of financing the CAP.

[17] See David Held, *Democracy and the Global Order: from the modern state to cosmopolitan governance*, Cambridge: Polity Press, 1995, pp. 107-22. Held also explains the process by which the use of public power has become 'internationalised' and why that process is, moreover, no less

irreversible and progressive in effect than the supranational provisions of the European Community treaties. See also D. Archibugi and D. Held (eds), *Cosmopolitan Democracy: an agenda for a new world order*, Cambridge: Polity Press, 1995; and Susan Strange, 'The Limits of Politics' in *Government and Opposition*, vol. 30, no. 3, 1995.

Chapter 4

[18] See Luigi Bonanate, 'Peace or Democracy' in Archibugi and Held op. cit.

[19] See Murray Forsyth, *Unions of States: the theory and practice of confederation*, Leicester: Leicester University Press, especially pp. 31-32.

[20] Ibid.

[21] See Samuel H. Beer, *To Make a Nation: the rediscovery of American federalism*, Cambridge, Mass.: Harvard, 1994. There are many more examples of federalism applied, over the past two centuries, which add to the complexity, including several originating in British overseas dominions in search of self-government and separate identity, as well as the almost euphemistic usage of the term 'federal' to classify what are effectively sovereign states formally constituted by distinct territorial entities that retain their own significant powers and forms of government (often themselves also confusingly named as 'states'). The Swiss confederation as constituted in 1848 (named as if to reflect the ambiguity typical of this topic) was the only case of a genuinely federal state in Europe to survive the nineteenth century; other experiments, like the German confederation, followed the path of national integration to become modern, virtually unitary, nation-states. Indeed, the search for an alternative to state sovereignty and the European imperial model was hardly commenced before being engulfed by the project of nationalism, most notably in the case of the USA, but even more savagely, in various European projects of modernisation imposed in the name of national integration (first the UK and France, then Germany and Italy). Experience during the present century, both in the USSR and in central and eastern European states that became subservient to a monolithic communist party, and even for different reasons in the postwar pluralistic federal republics of Germany and Austria, seem to confirm the judgement of both Preston King and Murray Forsyth that, besides relatively short-lived international confederations (*sic*), federalism as applied in conditions where the nation-state prevails has so far resulted only in what are effectively unitary forms of government, qualified only by the entrenchment of certain subsidiary rights of territorial communities to self-government. Forsyth, op. cit. and 'The political theory of federalism: the relevance of classical approaches', in Joachim Hesse and Vincent Wright (eds), *Federalizing Europe?* Oxford: Oxford University Press,

1996, pp. 24-45; Preston King, *Federalism and Federation*, London: Croom Helm, 1982.

[22] See in particular the critique of federalism as a doctrine of balance in King op. cit., pp. 56-68, especially page 62. The American federalists' critique of this aspect of what later became 'anti-federalism' was that 'balance' in itself cannot offer any particular benefit, unless balance and therefore stagnation be themselves the things most highly valued, in which case a precious safeguard against tyranny, faction, corruption and other usurpations of public virtue will have been foregone - namely, the possibility of intervention from outside the state or other forces of change.

[23] Beer, op. cit., p. 224. See also Paul Gillespie, 'Models of Integration' in Brigid Laffan (ed.), *Constitution-Building in the European Union*, Dublin: Institute of European Affairs, 1996, pp. 140-69.

[24] Alan S. Milward, *The European Rescue of the Nation-State*, London: Routledge, 1992; et. al., *The Frontier of National Sovereignty: history and theory, 1945-1992*, London: Routledge,1994.

[25] J.H.H. Weiler, 'Does Europe need a constitution? Demos, Telos, Ethos in the German Maastricht Decision' in *European Law Journal*, vol. 1, no. 3, 1995.

[26] See King, op. cit.

[27] See R.B.J. Walker, 'Gender and critique in the theory of international relations' in V. Spike Peterson (ed.), *Gendered States: feminist (re)visions of international relations theory*, Boulder, Col.: Lynne Reiner, 1992; Habermas (1981), op. cit., vol. 1, pp. 152-87; and Edmund Husserl, trans. David Carr, *The Crisis of European Sciences and Transcendental Phenomenology*, Evanston, Ill.: Northwestern University Press, 1970.

Chapter 5

[28] See Dieter Grimm, 'Does Europe need a constitution?' in *European Law Journal*, vol. 1, no. 3, 1995; and Weiler op. cit.

[29] Soledad Garcia (ed.), *European Identity and the Search for Legitimacy*, London: Pinter/RIIA, 1993; Brigid Laffan, 'The Politics of Identity and Political Order in Europe' in *Journal of Common Market Studies*, vol. 34, no. 1, 1996, pp. 81-102; Anthony Smith, 'National Identity and the Idea of European Unity' in *International Affairs*, vol. 68, no. 1, 1992; Ole Waever, 'Insécurité, identité: une dialectique sans fin', in Anne-Marie Le Gloannec (ed.), *Entre Union et Nations: L'État et L'Europe,* Paris: Presses de Sciences Politiques, 1998; and Dominique Wolton, *Naissance de l'Europe Démocratique*, Paris: Flammarion, 1993, pp. 299-360.

[30] Milward, op. cit.

[31] See Wolton, op. cit., especially pp. 247-54 & 399-404; Michael Newman, *Democracy, Sovereignty and the European Union*, London:

Hurst, 1996, pp. 173-200; Grimm, op.cit; Milward op. cit. (1993); Waever, op. cit.

[32] For a thorough investigation into the role of European lobbies, see Sonia Mazey and Jeremy Richardson, *Lobbying in the European Community,* Oxford: Oxford University Press, 1993; and for the general relevance of this aspect of political representation Jeremy Richardson, *European Union: power and policy-making in Western Europe*, London: Routledge, 1996.

[33] See Anthony Giddens, *Modernity and Self-identity: self and society in the late modern age*, Cambridge: Polity Press, 1991, especially pp. 209-31; Ulrike Beck, *The Re-Invention of Politics*, Cambridge: Polity Press, 1997; and Elizabeth Meehan, *Citizenship and the European Community*, London: Sage, 1993.

Chapter 6

[34] Hence the futility for this purpose of a study like Jean Blondel, Richard Sinnott and Palle Svensson, *People and Parliament in the European Union: Participation, Democrcay and Legitimacy*, Oxford: Clarendon Press, 1998.

[35] Held, op.cit., p. 147.

[36] Held, op. cit., pp. 157-93.

[37] Giandomenico Majone, *Regulating Europe*, London: Routledge, 1996.

[38] See Fritz Scharpf, 'The joint-decision trap: lessons from German federalism and European integration' in *Public Administration*, no. 66, 1988, pp. 239-78; 'Community and autonomy: multilevel policy-making in the European Union' in *Journal of European Public Policy*, no. 1, 1994, pp. 219-42; 'Can there be a stable federal balance in Europe?' in Hesse and Wright, op. cit., pp. 361-73 [1996a]; 'Negative and Positive Integration in the Political Economy of European Welfare States', in G. Marks et. al., *Governance in the European Union*, London: Sage, 1996 [1996b].

[39] See Andrew Duff, 'Superstate Euroland?' in Andrew Duff (ed.), *Understanding the Euro*, Foreword by Kenneth Clarke, London: Federal Trust with Kogan Page, 1998, especially pp. 155-56.

[40] Member states are bound by the objectives of the CFSP, though these are couched in such broad terms that it would be difficult to imagine any European state needing or wanting to deviate from them. Member states are also formally bound by the procedures of CFSP, including obligations to inform, consult and cooperate with one another on any matter of general interest, and to implement any consequent decisions, which might be taken by a qualified majority vote. Nevertheless, it is difficult to imagine any of the major states, or even a large number of the minor ones, being obliged to take some action, or even to desist from some action, against their will, especially since procedurally there continues,

even after Amsterdam, to be a national veto on majority voting and notwithstanding the possibility, introduced at Amsterdam, of constructive abstention.

[41] The Union has, of course, no military resources at its disposal except those belonging to its member states, most of which are already committed anyway to Nato, despite the WEU, which could hardly act on the instructions of the Union's Council, on the basis of a proposal from the Commission, or a recommendation of Parliament, contrary to, or even without the prior consent of, the Atlantic Council. The Commission can realistically propose economic action, friendly or hostile, but only when it can be certain of the support of enough of the economically stronger member states to make the action effective, and also surely only when it can be equally certain that the action and its repercussions will not seriously, and inequitably, harm the economically weaker members.

Chapter 7

[42] David Coombes, *The Future of the European Parliament*, London: Policy Studies Institute, European Series No. 1, 1979. I suggested that, if empirical comparisons were to be made then the European Parliament might be compared better with the House of Representatives of the US Congress, at least from an historical perspective, since there are similarities in the political and constitutional, as well as merely physical, circumstances. However, given people's extreme suggestibility in today's media-driven world, even that comparison is dangerous.

[43] For reasons in terms of public policy why this is so, see especially Scharpf op. cit., 1994, 1996a, 1996b.

[44] See, for example, the unfortunate interview of the British Foreign Secretary, Robin Cook, by John Lloyd in the *New Statesman*, 14 August 1998.